They Lied! True Tales of ™

Pregnancy, Childbirth and Breastfeeding

**Funny,
Unexpected
Experiences that Sound
a Little Hard to Believe ...
but Oh, So True**

Printed in Canada.

National Library of Canada Catologuing in Publication

Kane, Theresa, 1959-
They Lied!: true tales of pregnancy, childbirth and breastfeeding / Theresa Kane ; illustrations by Tamara Talbot.

ISBN: 0-973-2978-0-8

1. Pregnancy – Humour. 2. Childbirth – Humour. 3. Breast feeding – Humour. I. Talbot, Tamara, 1970- II. Title.

PN6178.C3K362004   618.2'002'07   C2004-902285-7

Trademark Acknowledgements

Viva Voce Press Inc. has attempted to include trademark information for products, services and companies referred to in this guide. Although Viva Voce Press Inc. has made reasonable efforts in gathering this information, it cannot guarantee its accuracy.

All other brand names and product names used in this book are trademarks, registered trademarks, or trade names of their respective holders. Viva Voce Press Inc. is not associated with any product or vendor mentioned in this book.

Visit our Web site at www.vivavocepress.com for information on other titles and our writers' guidelines.

Warning and Disclaimer

This book and any of its stories are not intended as medical advice. They should not be used as a substitute for the services and advice of any health-care professional.

Publisher:	Theresa Kane
Senior Editor:	Gordon Kirkland
Book Design:	Tamara Talbot
All Cover & Interior Illustrations:	Tamara Talbot

To the oldest, new experience in the history of mankind —
and all the people who make it happen.

Acknowledgments

We would like to thank all of the people who took the time to submit a story for consideration in this book. As our call for submissions was answered, we were overwhelmed by the quality and quantity of the stories that were submitted. Narrowing them down to the ones that you find in these pages was certainly a daunting, difficult task, but ultimately an inspiring one. We offer a special thanks to the authors whose stories were selected. You have been generous with your time and talent and patient with our process.

We would like to thank two moms who helped, as only moms would. To Delise Nicole, who added extra punch to our title, and to Monique Kane, who dug into her knowledge of grammar and punctuation to proofread the first manuscript. Once the moms had done their jobs, we turned over the work to Andrea Lemieux, who contributed her eye for detail, and her ear for humor on the final manuscript. The finishing touches were left to Laurie Clark with her eagle eye in layout. And, the illustration process came to completion with several inspirational conversations with Julie Bertoia, a first-time mom and talented artist. With the creative side of things well underway, administrative support was provided by Laurie Campbell, whom we also thank.

We would also like to thank our partners, without whom we would not have had the opportunity to experience the topics discussed in this book. We would like to thank our parents for going through with us what we have gone through in our own quests to add branches to our family trees.

Finally, we want to thank our children, whose conception, arrival and midnight feedings gave us the stories from our own lives that prove, without a doubt, that life often delivers a little more than you expect — more work, more surprises and more laughter.

Table of Contents

Introduction

This book is the result of an idea that was born eight years ago at a baby shower for my soon-to-be firstborn son, Matthew. Most of the women at that shower were inquisitive, well-read professionals who were now experiencing the dream of having children for the first time. We had all planned our pregnancies, done our homework and felt totally ready for the experience of being moms. Me included. But over the course of the conversation, we all realized that there is only so much preparation you can do.

And then reality sets it. It isn't a reality full of dread and worry. And, none of us had had any difficult experiences to speak of. But we all had experiences that were different from our expectations. When we talked about it, we all realized that no one ever really talks about pregnancy and childbirth. And, when you really, truly talk about it, the experiences are priceless.

This book, built with the delightful contributions of over fifty authors from places as far-reaching as New Zealand, South Africa, Canada, Ireland and the United States, is our attempt to share that reality. The funny, offbeat experiences that you never read about in a pregnancy manual. These are the defining moments that make each pregnancy unique, memorable and likely to bring tears of laughter down your cheeks. This book is a celebration of the absurd things that all of us experience in the name of having children.

While the concept was born at a shower, this book came to life as its creative team was assembled. I had the good fortune of being joined by an extraordinary team who could, with a chuckle, remember some of their own experiences and recognized that many other people would have stories to share. Tamara Talbot offers a bizarre childbirth experience of her own, along with an extraordinary talent as an illustrator and designer. With the core team in place, Gordon Kirkland, syndicated columnist and humorist, found us and just jumped into the deep end, sharing his experience and, as one would guess, his humour.

It has been a pleasure to nurture this concept to life with this team.

On a final note, this book and any of its stories are not intended to be medical advice. They should not be used as a substitute for the services and advice of any health-care providers. They are not meant to express a recommended way to duplicate or avoid any of the experiences described. They are not the recommended way to nurse, give birth, conceive or do anything else. They are just meant to make you laugh.

Live! Laugh! Enjoy it — all of it!

— *Theresa Kane*

Part One

Hey!
This Isn't What I Expected

For a few moments, I was not a mother-to-be. I was not a wife. I was simply a woman.

Girl Interrupted

By Sheri Guyse

When I was five months pregnant, my husband and I decided to take one last trip as a couple before we became a family. It was May and I had just finished my spring classes at the local college — I really needed a break and my husband needed some downtime before a busy summer at his job. We decided our best choice for some carefree fun would be Las Vegas.

Oklahoma, where we reside, is quite pleasant in May. The weather is breezy and just starting to get warm. Except for the occasional tornado or torrential thunderstorm, it is lovely. I thought that Las Vegas, with its eternal sunshine, would be just as lovely.

Boy, was I wrong.

Our shoulders seared as we scurried from casino to casino. We were flame-broiled poolside. All I wanted to do when we visited the dolphins at the Mirage was coax them to squirt chilly tank water from their blowholes to soothe my frictioned thighs.

By early afternoon each day, I had to rest. A nap in our room was my oasis in the Nevada desert. My husband was welcome to join me, watch some pay-per-view or head back to the casino — I really didn't care. But I had to sleep.

On one of those days, while we were basking during our cool siesta, things became a little frisky. What started out as a few loving kisses quickly became intense foreplay. I had read in all of my pregnancy bibles that around the fifth month of pregnancy a woman becomes a sex kitten.

This was not entirely correct.

Ironically, my enjoyment of sex had increased while my actual desire for it had gone kaput. Days upon days would pass before the slightest interest would arise. The books advised that I would feel like a sensual life-creating goddess and that all the new blood flow to my baby would make other things in that general area want to explode.

On this facet, though, they were quite correct.

My husband slowly kissed down my body, enjoying every new curve. I enjoyed feeling my rare sexual desire increase with each soft touch. Saying that my skin seemed to taste sweeter since my pregnancy, his lips brushed further down until he was in that general area I mentioned before. I lay back on the king-size bed and enjoyed all his mouth had to offer me. I breathed deeply and my hands stroked the crisp, white sheets.

For a few moments, I was not a mother-to-be. I was not a wife. I was simply a woman.

Suddenly, things heated. I could feel a warmth begin to burn on my thighs and a tingle shoot up my back. He sensed it too and became even more intent on my pleasure. My body started to squirm and I knew what was about to happen.

Or did I?

Without warning, a competitor entered the race for my long-awaited orgasm. I knew that all those Las Vegas bargain buffet binges came at a price; I just wasn't fully aware what kind of impact would befall my pregnant body. I eagerly approached the tiptop of my climax. Right as I was about to explode in pleasure, instant karma struck.

I farted.

In my husband's face.

He burst into wild laughter as I rolled over and sobbed uncontrollably. I cried for the loss of my old sexual self and I cried out of sheer frustration for the loss of the only orgasm I'd had in weeks. I cried because I was being a baby. I cried because I was having a baby. Then I cried because my husband, with a bewildered look on his face, tried to comfort me.

The blubbering eventually turned into embarrassed giggles as I reigned in control of my pregnancy hormones. For the rest of our trip to Sin City, I was not "Honey" or "Sugar" to my husband.

I was "Toots."

The Ten Biggest, Fattest Pregnancy Lies Exposed

By Megan Kelley Hall

Congratulations, you're pregnant! You may have visions of knitting booties as you curl up by a cozy fire, your cute little bump protruding sweetly beneath your stylish belly-bearing maternity top. Or perhaps you are looking forward to month after month of eating for two — all of the delicious, calorie-laden treats you usually pass over in order to keep your jeans from getting snug.

WRONG!

All of the fantasies of dream pregnancies that you've been floated by well-meaning friends, parents and loved ones are going to be dragged out into the light of day and proven to be one big fat lie after another. The deceptive images of pregnant women looking happy, content and well rested do not give a completely accurate view of pregnancy, as we know it. We've decided to expose the biggest and the fattest of all of the pregnancy lies to give a clear picture of what a pregnancy is REALLY like.

Big Fat Lie #1

You have a pregnancy glow.

That's sweat, thank you very much. Pregnant women work up more than just a glow when lugging around an extra thirty to fifty pounds. A glow is something you get after lounging in the sun on an exotic island or after a romantic romp with your lover. No, you were just caught coming from the bathroom after losing your lunch, yet again. Or perhaps you worked up a sweat while at battle with your closet trying to find something in between maternity clothes (you're not ready for those yet!) and your regular wardrobe (will you ever squeeze into those sizes again?).

At least they noticed something besides your huge, bulging midsection.

Big Fat Lie #2
You may have a touch of morning sickness.

Morning sickness? Sounds pretty harmless, doesn't it? Awww, she has a little bit of morning sickness. Isn't that sweet? Let's just call it morning, noon and night sickness, or 24-7 madness, because that's how you feel after being plagued with this illness for three months (some lucky girls even have it throughout their entire pregnancy!). For those who've never experienced "morning sickness," imagine a hangover that never goes away, or being stuck on a boat during a storm after consuming an array of deviled eggs, smoked bacon and cheap champagne.

Try a touch of that and see how cute you feel.

Big Fat Lie #3
Nothing's more beautiful than a pregnant woman.

That may be, but nothing feels less attractive. Your hair is greasy, your body is expanding at an alarming rate, you are physically and mentally exhausted and you're sick all the time. Now what could make anyone feel more beautiful than that? Sure, you have great cleavage (something that many of us have waited for since puberty), but no one mentioned that your breasts ache all the time. Great. The first time in your life that you have a huge chest and you can't even enjoy it. If anyone so much as grazes the area, you may have cause to kill.

Big Fat Lie #4
You'll get a big, beautiful belly.

Sure you do. But nobody told you about the big old butt that you'll get to match. Or how about those charming flabby arms and thick sausage legs? When you think pregnant, you think belly, right? Wrong. Your whole body is super-sized. Plus, most women spend their entire lives self-conscious about their body size then, all of a sudden, it becomes acceptable for people, even complete strangers, to comment on how big you're getting. They even feel compelled to invade your personal space by grabbing at your stomach. Don't hesitate to tell them to back away and keep their hands off. And while you're at it, ask them how many pounds they've packed on recently. See how *they* like it.

Big Fat Lie #5

You can eat whatever you want.

Now this part sounds great. What they don't tell you, however, is that most of the time you'll be too sick to eat anything at all. Sure, you can put away cartons of Ben and Jerry's ice cream and eat all the chocolate bars you want. Problem is that most pregnant moms can barely stomach animal crackers and dry toast. Plus, there are millions of foods you can't eat because they put the baby at risk. Say good-bye to grilled swordfish and Caesar salads. No more Brie cheese and ham slices for you, mommy-to-be. And once your food aversions and "morning sickness" let up, there's all that pressure to eat healthy for the new baby. It was hard enough to eat responsibly when it was just you, but now there's another entire person depending on whether or not you have a baked potato on the side (no thanks) or fries (yes, please!).

Big Fat Lie #6

It's only nine months. It will fly by before you know it.

Actually, it's closer to ten months, or forty weeks, or 280 days. That's practically an entire school year of being pregnant. But no one tells you that until it happens to you. And, no, it doesn't fly by. It is slow and gradual, each day bringing with it new obstacles and problems to overcome. Ten months of giving up your favorite foods, your entire wardrobe (good-bye, high heels and designer clothes, hello, muu-muus and sweats), your social life (who has the energy to stay out late?), your sex life (some pregnancies require abstinence as you get closer to the due date — surprise, surprise) and your daily dose of caffeine.

If men had to give up sex, junk food, coffee, beer, parties and generally feeling good for practically a year with the big payoff being an excruciatingly painful delivery, procreation would screech to an immediate halt.

Big Fat Lie #7

It'll be easy to maintain your fitness program during pregnancy.

It was hard to get motivated to work out before pregnancy. Now, all of a sudden that you've doubled your weight and can't even see your Nikes to tie them, you're supposed to be first in line for the Stairmaster at your local gym? I don't think so. Besides, what's the point of working out when it will be at least a year before you see any results? Most pregnant women get winded just walking up and down the stairs carrying an extra thirty-pound weight with them wherever they go. That's more than enough exercise for me, thank you very much.

Big Fat Lie #8

You'll be back to your prepregnancy weight in no time.

Do yourself a favor right now. Do not, under any circumstances, pay attention to how quickly celebrity moms return to their prepregnancy weight. Some even appear to have a pact with the devil and end up in better shape than they were before they got pregnant. This is very depressing and misleading to the significant others of nonfamous pregnant ladies. Make sure that you realize that the weight will come off in time, but plan on sporting your maternity clothes a bit longer than you anticipated. And please don't be one of those women. You know who I'm talking about — the ones that can fit into their jeans a day after the delivery.

No offense, but we hate you.

Big Fat Lie #9

You can make labor easier with breathing techniques.

Yup, and you can make a severed arm feel better by whistling Zippity-Doo-Dah. Many experts advise that you focus on your breath during delivery to help you manage the discomfort. What they don't tell you is that it's impossible to focus on anything but the excruciating pain emanating from an area that most women are a bit shy about, but which is now on display for the world to see.

Focus on this: pain bad, breathing good, painkillers even better.

Hey! This Isn't What I Expected

Big Fat Lie #10

It'll all be worth it in the end.

Sure it will, but who wants to go through nine months (I'm sorry, did I say nine, make that ten months) of hell to get there? And when the day finally arrives, it's not all teddy bears and flowers and balloons. It is a long, painful and not very pretty process of delivering a baby. (I won't spoil it for you now — you'll find out soon enough what kind of craziness your body goes through on the big day. Ladies, trust me, leave your video cameras at home.)

Then again, once you look into the eyes of this beautiful little person that you've created — a baby that wouldn't be in the world if it hadn't been protected and carried and nurtured inside you for these past nine months — you realize that maybe, just maybe, this isn't a pregnancy lie.

Maybe this is the biggest and most important truth of all.

No Small Potatoes

By Amanda Euringer

Everyone knows that there are cultural differences between the east and west coasts of North America. In the east, we have New York, Toronto and Montreal. Think: smoking, great art and universities, smoked meat and burgers. On the west coast, we have L.A, Seattle and Vancouver. Think: bad TV, health fanatics and tofu eaters. These may seem like small differences, but the culture shock of moving from one end to the other can be overwhelming.

I had been living in British Columbia for only about a year when I became pregnant, and I decided that I should embrace my new culture and be a mom the West-Coast way. To me this meant finding midwives and a doula (or nursing coach — very West Coast), joining a prenatal yoga class and cutting out alcohol and red meat.

I was proud of myself. Look how far I had come. I was a West Coaster!

As my belly grew rounder I noticed that complete strangers felt free to ask me very personal questions about myself, and to freely give lots of candid advice on parenting and birthing.

Most of these questions were standard: "How many months pregnant are you?" which was often followed by, "Really? You must be having twins," or, "It's a girl because you're really carrying the weight ALL OVER" and, "Do you know what you are having?" (Clearly, an elephant.) But, on the west coast the clear favorite, which even small, gray-haired grandmas on the bus would ask me, was:

"What are you going to do with your placenta?"

"My what?" I asked uncertainly the first time.

The woman at my yoga class smiled at me in a deprecating way and began speaking more slowly and loudly — the way you might speak to your old aunt, or a rather dumb child.

"YOUR PLA-CEN-TA," she smiled again, and wafted her

patchouli-scented hair away from her face.

I looked at her blankly, trying in vain to remember tenth-grade biology.

She stretched her arms over perfectly tanned, and still slender, legs.

"You know, your baby's little sac. Her home that she's growing in. I am going to plant mine in the backyard under our apple tree."

She was wearing short boy shorts and a tank top; her perfectly round, tanned tummy didn't have a single stretchmark on it.

I tried not to hate her. I faked an "Ohhhhh … the placenta, of course . . . right. Good for you," and a "How nice . . . an apple tree," before giving up on ever touching my toes and making for the bathroom.

My placenta?

As far as I knew, I had never heard of anyone making plans for their baby's "sac" before. Frankly, I was a little embarrassed for the woman and sat next to a nice yuppie-looking mom when I returned.

And then, it happened again.

And, AGAIN.

West-Coast people were planting their placentas under trees, burning them, and spreading their ashes somewhere with a nice view of the mountains. Perfectly nice, normal-looking people offered me recipes they had used to cook their placentas.

"In the wild, women need the nutrients," they would say in explanation.

"Yes, but we have husbands," I would suggest, "and grocery stores."

Always, I would get the same look of pity, as if I was some-how missing a great opportunity to bond with my baby's "little home."

The final straw came when a well-meaning man offered me instructions on how to make a dream catcher out of it. He'd made one for his child.

"No!" I screamed in a nine-month-pregnant angry rage, "NO! I will not be doing anything special with my placenta. Is that okay? Can I still live here, or do I need to go back to Toronto. I am NOT going to bond in any way with my baby's sac. I am not interested in my baby's sac. I …"

I was still screaming, and the poor man was slowly trying to inch himself away from me at the supermarket where we were both shopping. "I am only interested in bonding with THE BABY. I will keep THE BABY and THROW OUT the PLA-CEN-TA, like every normal person east of the Rockies!"

The man practically ran out of the supermarket, and my smug response to any questions concerning my placenta was, "Into the garbage!" from then on.

Now, no one had told me that you have to give birth to the placenta AFTER you have just spent twelve pain-filled hours giving birth to your child. After finally having pushed out my perfectly formed daughter (along with a few unmentionable items that floated none too prettily in my birthing pool.) My feelings turned into panic when I started feeling more contractions.

"What was that?" I snapped at my midwife, as if it was somehow her fault, "Why am I feeling pain?"

"Oh," said my midwife, gently massaging the shoulder that I had inadvertently bitten during my very West-Coast, no painkiller, water birth, "That's your placenta. You still have to give birth to it. It shouldn't hurt too much."

I tried to keep the pleading sound out of my voice, "But, but I don't want to feel any more pain."

"Oh, it will be over in no time," she said, assuming the classic catcher position. "Just concentrate on your new girl."

I concentrated on my new girl.

"Whew, just look at the size of this thing." The midwife sounded truly excited.

I concentrated on my girl.

"Hey, Marie," she called the other midwife into the room, "Have you ever seen one this big before?"

The other midwife actually let out a low whistle of appreciation,

Hey! This Isn't What I Expected

"That is one huge, healthy placenta. It must weigh at least a couple of pounds."

I tried to concentrate on my baby.

"You gotta see this thing," my midwife said to me, "Do you want to see it?"

My husband got up and went over to take a look, "Honey, this thing is amazing. You really should check it out."

I lost concentration on my baby.

"No. I do not want to see my placenta, abnormally huge or not. Now could you please, JUST THROW IT OUT!"

The room was dead silent, even the baby had stopped fussing. My husband carefully approached me and began rubbing my back, while making appropriate "what a huge and perfect baby you just made" comments, and the midwives slunk out of the room with the award-winning placenta.

A week later, when I was up and about, I was peering into the fridge looking for something to eat (no one had told me that breastfeeding moms are just as hungry as pregnant moms), when I pulled out a large, double-sized yogurt container full to the brim with something that looked like a suspicious cross between liver and a brain. I was confused. My partner was a vegetarian and he had been doing all the shopping that week. I certainly had never bought anything that looked like that.

"Umm, honey, what's this delightful stuff you have hidden in the extra large bucket of plain yogurt?"

My husband gave a look I usually only got from my dog and said, "That's your placenta." He hurried on before I could get angry, "The midwives said that you can't just throw them into the garbage, they have to be taken away and burned.

It's related to the same laws that make you properly dispose of dead bodies. Anyway, it has to be taken away to the hospital and incinerated in a special oven, but they can't do that until it has umm … ripened … a bit because it won't burn properly, or something. I don't know exactly. We were trying to whisper so that you wouldn't be upset and I missed some of the conversation."

"Are you telling me that people can EAT their placentas, or dry them, but that we can't throw this into the garbage?"

"Yes. And the midwives are coming tomorrow so we can give it to them. Okay?"

I nodded and put the placenta back in the fridge. It really was huge. But the midwives never came.

So, there it sat: My placenta in a yogurt container. Blending beautifully with all the rest of the fridge items. Camouflaged.

Can you see where this is going?

A month passed, then two. We were busy with our new baby and no sleep. By the time we thought about it again, I was too embarrassed to send it to the hospital. "Hi, here is the two-month-old placenta we have had sitting in our fridge." No stranger should have to deal with that.

"Honey?" I said, handing my husband the container, "this has become your job. I gave birth to our child, you throw this in the garbage."

"I can't," he said, pushing the container back at me. "What if someone finds out?"

"What? You think the placenta police are going to catch you?"

"Well, it's just that the midwives said …"

"Do you want to take it to the hospital?" I said, gingerly holding the bucket away from me.

"NO."

"Well, then," I said, thrusting the container back in his direction, "into the garbage."

Grumbling, he took the container out of my hands and balanced it on top of the railing on the back porch, "I'll take it out tomorrow when I go."

Well, it was winter, and in the winter we never used the back porch in our house.

Yup, another month passed.

One night, when my girl was nearly four months old and spring had poked its wet nose out of the frosty ground, there was a knock on the back-porch door. My husband and I looked at each other. No one had ever knocked on our back door before.

Hey! This Isn't What I Expected

"Must be the organic delivery guy," I surmised. I had just begun receiving weekly grocery deliveries from my favorite organics company.

My husband got up to answer the door and I heard a very small, frightened, male voice say,

"I'm sorry to disturb you but I just knocked … I knocked … um … something off the railing of your porch … and … and …"

Both my husband and I realized in the same horrifying moment what had happened.

"Oh, don't worry, it's okay," I could hear my partner scrambling to put this terrified, probably vegetarian, twenty-something, organic delivery guy at ease,

"My wife just had a baby and that's her umm, it's her …" He was panicking. I jumped in to help, but couldn't remember the word myself so I shouted out,

"My uterus!"

"Yeah, it's okay," my husband said, smiling reassuringly, "t's just her uterus."

That night, under cover of darkness, my husband and I buried my placenta under the big cedar in our backyard. Although we still receive organic groceries, I have never seen another delivery guy in person. I think they sneak up to our house and throw the groceries on our steps and run away, hoping never to have to see us again.

But every time I look at that cedar tree, I have to smile.

I guess I'm on the West Coast to stay.

A Breastfeeding Annual Report

By Jamie M. Pearson

"Your husband should buy you some jewelry," confided my girlfriend as she fished a bottle from her diaper bag and shook it vigorously.

She had just weaned her baby and was still reeling from the high cost of formula. "You're saving him a fortune."

"I don't know about that." I gazed at my peacefully suckling son, "But it's so much easier."

A small white lie.

Although I would never use formula myself, I supported my friend's decision. I did not consider her a lesser mother for choosing an easier path. Then, as if on cue, my son bit me.

Hard.

Hard enough to make my ears ring from the pain. Hard enough that I yelped in anguish and launched the little bloodsucker off my lap. This didn't do much for my beatific nursing-mother image. As I blinked back tears, I wondered if the bite wasn't instant karma.

Breastfeeding gets great press. Advocates deliver a consistent, if slightly monotonous message, "It's nutritious, rewarding, cheap and easy."

Nutritious? The evidence is irrefutable.

Rewarding? In my experience, the physical intimacy of nursing can be breathtaking.

Cheap and easy? Not so fast.

Remember, these are the same people who told us if your baby is latched on properly, breastfeeding doesn't hurt. It's almost as if breastfeeding advocates don't trust us with the truth.

Sometimes nursing sucks.

Breastfeeding was one of the seminal experiences of my life, but it tested me. Both times. Despite unanticipated costs and

Hey! This Isn't What I Expected

painful complications, I stuck it out. Just because it's what nature intended doesn't mean it was easy.

Or cheap.

The following is a month-by-month annual report of the year I spent breastfeeding my son. For cost comparison, I polled ten formula-savvy friends about bottle-feeding. Some used expensive hypoallergenic formula and elaborate bottle sterilization systems. Others bought in bulk and hoarded coupons. Their average annualized monthly outlay was $95.

Here's how my own expenses and experiences stacked up.

February

Late pregnancy splurge-fest begets astronomical one-time start-up costs.

- Time-saving electric breast pump ($300).
- Nursing pads ($10).
- Fascinating new toys to keep toddler from climbing on the head of nursing newborn ($40).

Hypothetical cost of formula:	$ 0
Actual cost of breastfeeding:	$350
Money saved by breastfeeding:	-$350

March

Baby Max arrives! Nursing bras from last time stretch and strain in fruitless effort to accommodate painfully engorged size 36DD breasts that also arrive.

- New bra, priority overnight shipping ($60).
- Lanolin ointment for excruciatingly sore nipples ($8).
- Fascinating new videos to keep toddler from climbing on the head of nursing newborn ($30).
- Nursing pads ($10).

Hypothetical cost of formula:	$ 95
Actual cost of breastfeeding:	$108
Money saved by breastfeeding:	-$ 13

April

I'm besieged by clogged milk ducts. My nursing enthusiasm dwindles. I desperately need spare nursing bra in order to be able to occasionally wash existing nursing bra.

- Congratulate self for spending less this time ($17).
- Nursing pads ($10).

Hypothetical cost of formula:	$ 95
Actual cost of breastfeeding:	$ 27
Money saved by breastfeeding:	$ 68

May

- Replace cheap, chafing, uncomfortable spare nursing bra with expensive, chafing, uncomfortable spare nursing bra ($50).
- Nursing pads ($10).

Hypothetical cost of formula:	$ 95
Actual cost of breastfeeding:	$ 60
Money saved by breastfeeding:	$ 35

June

Nipples become inexplicably tender, nursing painful. Unfortunate combination of warm weather and outlandishly large breasts prompts emergency shopping trip.

- Assortment of shirts, size XL ($100).
- Nursing pads ($10).

Hypothetical cost of formula:	$ 95
Actual cost of breastfeeding:	$110
Money saved by breastfeeding:	-$ 15

Hey! This Isn't What I Expected

July

Nipples become inexplicably tender, nursing painful. Unfortunate combination of warm weather and outlandishly large breasts prompts emergency shopping trip.

- Lactation consultant for astonishing nursing pain, nipples now cracked and bleeding ($125).
- Consultant diagnoses thrush, a yeast infection passed back and forth between nursing mothers and babies. Various medications for thrush ($20).
- Nursing pads ($10).

Hypothetical cost of formula:	$ 95
Actual cost of breastfeeding:	$155
Money saved by breastfeeding:	-$ 60

August

Thrush improves somewhat, yet lingers.

- New medicine ($10).
- Nursing pads ($10).

Hypothetical cost of formula:	$ 95
Actual cost of breastfeeding:	$ 20
Money saved by breastfeeding:	$ 75

September

I have quite possibly invented new, medicine-resistant strain of thrush. I am the Marie Curie of breast infections.

- Two more new medicines ($12).
- Nursing pads ($10).

Hypothetical cost of formula	$ 95
Actual cost of breastfeeding:	$ 22
Money saved by breastfeeding:	$ 73

October

Thrush finally clears up. Max mysteriously refuses to nurse on the right side. This costs nothing, but resulting freakish appearance tests commitment to breast feeding. Consider surrendering. Consider joining the circus.

- Nursing pads ($10).

Hypothetical cost of formula:	$ 95
Actual cost of breastfeeding:	$ 10
Money saved by breastfeeding:	$ 85

November
Weather turns colder. Am noticeably lopsided. Tight sweaters absolutely out of the question.
- New, looser sweaters ($125).
- Nursing pads ($10).

Hypothetical cost of formula:	$ 95
Actual cost of breastfeeding:	$135
Money saved by breastfeeding:	-$ 40

December
With the advent of teeth comes a brief, yet excruciating biting phase. Unbelievably, the pain of thrush pales by comparison. Somehow I survive this dental reign of terror.
- New holiday party outfit to disguise ridiculous size 36DD physique ($100).
- Nursing pads ($10).

Hypothetical cost of formula:	$ 95
Actual cost of breastfeeding:	$110
Money saved by breastfeeding:	-$ 15

January
Max begins scratching and pinching my neck like a crazed kitten while nursing. Refuses to nurse when restrained. Actually manages to draw blood.
- Turtlenecks for protection ($40).
- Nursing pads ($10).

Hypothetical cost of formula:	$ 95
Actual cost of breastfeeding:	$ 50
Money saved by breastfeeding:	$ 45

Hey! This Isn't What I Expected

February

I am overwhelmed by irrational melancholy as I begin the weaning process. Feel nostalgia for this fleeting physical connection between us. Max reaches up, lacerates unprotected neck with razor-sharp baby fingernails. Feel slightly less nostalgia for this fleeting physical connection between us.

Hypothetical cost of formula:	$ 95
Actual cost of breastfeeding:	$ 0
Money saved by breastfeeding:	$ 95

Hypothetically, I would have spent a total of $1,140 on formula. My breastfeeding expenditures came to $1,157. So much for cheap and easy.

And while the extra seventeen dollars I spent won't buy me the diamond tiara I so richly deserve, you can't put a price tag on my memories.

Babies and Boobies and Boisterous Boys, Oh My …

By Diane Meredith Vogel

I'm a firm believer in the benefits of breastfeeding and nursed all three of our children. A vocal proponent of the practice, I told anyone who would listen about all the nutritional and psychological benefits as well as the wonderful convenience of feeding babies, "the way God designed it to be done."

The baby of the family, Jessica, was a few months old and such a contented and mellow baby. She was a joy to take any place. It had been a while since we'd been out, and a new Disney movie was playing at a theater about twenty minutes from our home, so we planned a family night at the movie theater.

For the whole day, the two older children were filled with anticipation. They had seen the previews for the movie on television and were very excited about going to the show.

With the diaper bag packed, and the baby bathed and dressed in her pajamas so we could put her right to bed when we got home, we were off.

We got a great, close parking space and the line at the ticket booth was short and moved fast. It seemed like it would be a great night. We went into the theater and got our seats. Then the two older children went with their daddy on a popcorn quest.

Mission accomplished, they all snuggled into their seats just as the house lights dimmed. For some reason, the sudden darkness roused the baby who had been sleeping peacefully in my arms. She looked around with confusion in her eyes and then, WHAM!

The loud music announcing the coming attractions burst from the surround-sound speakers, startling little Jessie into a dramatic stiff-armed shudder.

She squealed and began to cry loudly. I tried to comfort her and shush her. I held her close and stroked her hair and cheek.

Hey! This Isn't What I Expected

She cried louder. I changed position and took off her little jacket, thinking she might be too warm.

Louder still.

When there was a momentary quiet between two of the previews, Jessie took the opportunity to let go with a loud, mournful wail, and before the sound system roared back to life, everyone in attendance heard the voice of our son, then five, and obviously quite exasperated.

He stood up, which made the sound of his little boy voice carry even farther than normal. Placing a concerned hand on my knee, he said loudly, with perfect diction and his clear-as-a-bell voice, "Give her a boob, Mom. Try a boob!"

Though the preview was not for a comedy, the theater was filled with laughter.

Part Two

Taking All the Fun
Out of Sex

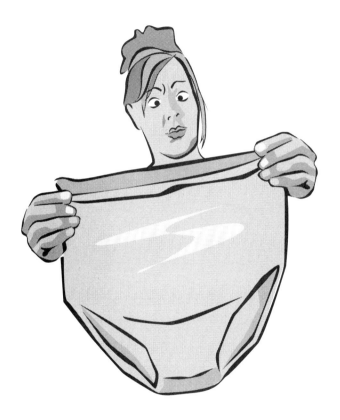

*It shouldn't have been a surprise
that Richard was not aroused.
I wasn't exactly an encouraging
Mae West.*

Half Mast

By Jennifer D. Munro

Richard and I stood naked and droopy in our bedroom on the appointed evening when we were to fornicate under doctor's orders.

We had to get up early for work the next morning. The dog needed walking. The laundry basket overflowed. We simply wanted to get the prescription procreation over with so we could fall asleep. This presented more of a challenge for my husband than for me. I just needed to lie there and be a human receptacle, whereas Richard needed to give the performance of a lifetime.

On cue …

My husband and I had been at the beck and call of my ovaries for half a year. A slew of tests, almost daily visits to the fertility specialists and the careful manipulation of my cycle through five kinds of hormonal drugs all led up to this momentous, orchestrated sex in order to conceive a much-wanted child.

The doctor had finally decreed that my uterine lining was ideal. My estrogen level was right on target. My follicle size was perfect. All that remained was a full frontal assault on the hapless egg.

But judging by the drooping flag, my husband's private soldier had turned pacifist.

Richard had been the passive participant up until now. He accompanied me to numerous doctor appointments for moral support, but his role was limited to watching. He rubbernecked while experts poked and prodded to locate the source of my fertility problem. Sometimes he and the doctor put their heads together over the ultrasound screen like Bo and Luke Duke bent over the hood of a faulty car engine.

Now, in an instant, after months of idling in neutral, the doctor promoted him from thumb-twiddling passenger to pilot of the reproductive rocket ship. All systems were go. A rapid countdown began for Richard's sperm to take off into the regulated cosmos of my reproductive organs. His helmeted army must traverse my oviduct and conquer the single, perfect egg that hovered like a new moon on the ultrasound screen.

So after months of yawning while the doctor tracked and controlled my gonads, the medical team suddenly handed him the reins of my runaway egg. The follicle's unexpected growth spurt might cause it to burst before Richard's amphibious legion could swarm into estrogen territory. Used to watching the proverbial grass of my gametes grow, he had to spring into coital action.

A chipper medical assistant injected a follicle-rupturing hormone into my rump while my husband and an intern looked on, four of us crammed in a tiny exam room. They stared at the great round globe of my right haunch with rapt attention, as if, instead of a hyperbolic sinking into my cellulite craters, they were witnessing the Apollo moon landing.

She issued her final instructions: "Timed Intercourse."

"Now?" I pictured her with a stopwatch and checkered flag.

"Tonight's fine," she said cheerily, not looking at us as she disposed of the needle in a bin stuffed with used syringes, "and tomorrow, and the next day. Three times is preferable. But not absolutely necessary."

As a procreating robot undergoing tune-up, I felt anything but sexy. Richard was lucky if my teeth were brushed. I wanted to don my flannel nightie and read two paragraphs of my book before passing out, not engage in frisky shenanigans born not of lust for each other but of a doctor's dictate.

Where I could hide my dispassion, Richard could not.

It shouldn't have been a surprise that Richard was not aroused. I wasn't exactly an encouraging Mae West. The doctor had mixed a potent cocktail of synthetic hormones inside me for weeks, orchestrating my cycle. The drugs timed the release of pumped-up eggs that would hopefully produce a healthy baby who could bench press his own weight at birth. Unfortunately, the potion hadn't assaulted my reproductive organs alone. Equal Opportunity drugs, they sloshed freely into my brain cells, nerve endings and vocal cords.

I had the temper of an electrocuted cat: fur puffed out, claws extended, canines bared, profanities screeched.

Yield became the operative sign of my husband's life. Richard described hostile aliens occupying my body. He looked into my ear and asked, "Who's in there? Have you seen my wife?"

This didn't go over well, but I asked the same thing when I looked in mirrors. I wasn't relishing this mind-altering experiment with a personality disorder.

In my new role as Jaws, I had no patience for a wilting weenie.

Richard stood and waited. It's what he'd been trained to do up until now. He suddenly had to storm my castle with raised sword, but instead of Excalibur, he possessed a weird and fickle contraption called a penis, a device with a mind of its own and few operating instructions.

The innocent, hormone-free chickadee peeped in my ear, high on the treble clef, "Oral-sex, oral-sex, oral-sex."

Yes, subtle encouragement of the tender and erotic variety would have been the best solution to the immediate problem. But months of stress, the dehumanization of fertility treatment and the mood-warping drugs left me drained of generosity.

The aliens inside me screamed, "Fellatio, on top of everything else? Are you kidding? You think this Band-Aid on my butt is fun? You think leaking hormone suppositories on my panties is a turn-on? Who said anything about pleasure?"

I was worn out and empty, just a ticked-off shell for an exploding follicle.

I could have — should have — gone down on my knees in compassionate spirit and taken up the chalice of contrition. I could have elevated this moment to a sacred union of bodies that would create a miracle.

But I did not.

My version of foreplay went something like this: standing with arms crossed over bare breasts, foot tapping, rolling of eyes, exasperated sighs. "I've been in charge of everything else up until now. This is the only thing you've been asked to do.

"That," pointing at the offending member, "is your responsibility. Hurry up. I'm tired."

Richard wasn't experiencing anything that I wasn't. My arousal was about as likely to happen as weight loss during the holidays. Coitus on command, with so much at stake, under the microscope of a medical team, was not our version of kink. Those who knew we were actively pursuing pregnancy thought we were bumping all the time like hyperactive bunnies. Truthfully, we had never had less sex since the doctors had taken over my body.

There is nothing so unerotic as compulsory copulation.

Unable to progress under my caustic gaze after much shouting accusation, he retreated to the bathroom to elicit an enthusiastic response, most likely thinking of anything but his snarling wife. Not possessing similar mechanics, I imagine even the most sustained friction will force a reaction despite the protestation of the mind. Whatever the case, he returned in a state necessary to perform the heroic feat of fertilizing a monster.

When Richard someday arrives at the Pearly Gates, Peter will point to Richard's peter and say, "After you, dear boy," opening the door to heaven with a flourish. This was Richard's superlative moment of self-sacrificing love. Spurred on by my cries of "Get-it-up," he rode in, erect on his white horse and saved the day.

My period two weeks later came as no surprise. How could my selfishness have bred something joyous? But conceiving on our own a while later, with no doctors or drugs, just passion and love after the aliens returned my genial personality, did come as a pleasant surprise.

Sex, Lies and Measuring Tapes

By Yvonne Eve Walus

Ever since I can remember, my biggest pregnancy-related fear was not that of giving birth or losing my freedom to a bald, toothless stranger who doesn't speak a word of English. It was losing my sexuality.

I honestly don't know where I got the idea from, a naughty book or a horror movie. But planted firmly in my mind was the belief that once a baby slips through the birth canal, the vaginal walls are stretched out of proportion — forevermore beyond repair.

"Poppycock," my midwife pronounced. "I'm not letting you have an elective C-section just because you're scared of ending up like an old balloon. Women are perfectly capable of having sex after a vaginal delivery, trust me."

"Yeah," said a little voice inside me, "they may be capable of having sex, but do they get any fun out of it?"

You see, I consider myself somewhat of a sex bomb (even if others opt to reserve their judgment), and the thought of not meeting the criteria anymore was terrifying.

Well, the big occasion came and went, as they do. I was lucky to have a relatively quick labor (measured in hours as opposed to days), a non-instrumental vaginal delivery and no stitches afterward.

"Yes!" I thought. "All intact and ready to roll."

The baby seems to have no trouble sleeping. She's an hour old and already knows how to do it, so the nights will be ours to use as we please.

Then I went to have a shower and discovered something hanging between my legs. It felt like a scrotum. Upon a hasty mirror examination, I discovered that my perineum had stretched, and now looked indeed very much like an old balloon.

Of the attractive purple variety.

Needless to say, it took several weeks and several ice packs before I was ready to inspect my vagina again. By then, nothing resembled old balloons, so I decided to venture further and rediscover my sexuality.

"You may have sex as soon as you feel like it," the midwife had advised, "but use lots of lubricant."

So we did. My thighs were practically swimming in lubricating jelly. The ingress was slow and careful, and more than a tad painful, but I persevered, knowing the pleasures that surely awaited once I got into the swing of things.

And then it happened. There I was in the middle of my favorite activity, and I felt absolutely nothing. No pain. No pleasure. No penis, none that I was aware of anyway.

Now that presented a problem. I was taught that male egos are fragile things, and to say "Is it in, darling?" was always a highly inappropriate question. So how was I to register a complaint?

Fortunately, my husband's not used to my lying there like a dead fish without making a sound.

"What's wrong?" he asked.

"My G-spot went AWOL. I can't feel a thing."

"That's okay. Thirty percent of women don't even know where their
G-spot is."

So much for his being supportive. I didn't care about other women. I used to know where my G-spot was. And I wanted it back.

As you can imagine, my reintroduction to sex after pregnancy did not suffuse me with optimism for my old-balloon-like vagina, even though my husband insisted it didn't feel any different. It bloody did too!

To add insult to the injury, I still felt far from sexy. It was already two weeks since I'd lost thirteen pounds in one night (now there's an advantage to giving birth), and I wanted to lose more.

Taking All the Fun Out of Sex

Now, you know how they said that when you breastfeed you'd lose all the weight you'd put on during pregnancy?

They lied.

One actually gains weight when breastfeeding, especially if you take supplements to maintain your milk supply. And even when you do reach your prepregnancy weight, you still don't fit into your favorite jeans — your hips simply register two inches more on the measuring tape, and that's that.

So there I was — fat, with no G-spot, and with the sexual fantasy life of an amoeba. Because, you see, they didn't lie about the exhaustion aspect of having babies. You never sleep more than three hours at a time. Your arms feel ready to fall off from carrying the baby all day. Your back hurts from bending over the changing table. Your body feels like jelly and your brain is scattered.

My favorite fantasy at the moment goes like this: I check into a five-star hotel on a Friday night, all alone. I recline on the round bed and sip the complimentary champagne while I read the book I bought myself for Christmas but never got round to reading between breastfeeding and diaper changes. A gourmet meal is brought up to my room and I continue to read through the meal and later in the fragrant spa bath. Finally, I slip between the satin sheets and sleep for fifteen hours, totally uninterrupted.

My husband can join me in the morning for a bout of you-know-what, now that we've regained the G-spot.

But that's another fairy tale.

Egg

By Abby Lederman

I was adopted. My adopted mother had fertility problems, so I was lucky enough to enter her life as her baby girl. Twenty-seven years later, I was ready to have my own child when, to my utter amazement, I discovered that I had a fertility problem, too. No gene connection, but we had to wonder. Was it the air I breathed as a kid growing up in suburban Pound Ridge, New York?

My husband and I started frequenting the Infertility Clinic at the University of Pennsylvania. Everyone there assured me that they would solve our problem and I would conceive — we just had to keep trying.

Over the following two years, my husband and I paid many visits to the clinic. We did all the humiliating things that couples do when their future lies in the hands of fertility experts. My husband left warm specimens in bathrooms decked out with *Playboy*™ magazines. We had sex on a schedule. I religiously held my legs in the air for a half hour after the act. I got inseminated monthly in the office with my husband's plentiful but lazy sperm. (If only I had known, would I have married a man with lazy sperm?)

Finally fed up with all the brouhaha, we stopped worrying so much. All our friends, who were about ten years ahead of us in the parenting department, stopped asking us if there was any news. We continued to dream of a baby of our own, while looking into adoption. And then it happened. I missed a period, I started feeling nauseous and my breasts got rock hard. Could it be? I had been through so many disappointing pregnancy tests that I was afraid to even hope.

I took the test on the first day that it could be effective, so I believe I was about ten days late. When the results were positive, I was awestruck. I worked in an open office at the time, and I had to whisper in the phone to my husband.

"Positive," I told him discreetly.

Taking All the Fun Out of Sex

Then I heard him screaming to his co-workers, "It's positive," which meant he had already told everyone in the entire office building that I might be pregnant.

So much for discretion.

When I got home that night, my wonderful husband (of the slow but apparently reliable sperm) was waiting with sparkling grape juice and the first of perhaps several dozen greeting cards he managed to find for me featuring pictures of eggs.

Since neither of us had any sense at all, we got in our car and raced around the neighborhood, visiting all our friends to introduce them to our new baby, a baby we immediately nick-named "Egg."

The growth inside me couldn't have been more than a zygote at the time, but my husband proudly cupped my belly (back then there wasn't much to cup) and proclaimed, "I want you to "meet Egg."

For the next nine months, our poor social group was forced to hear of every accomplishment of our child, Egg. When I felt sick due to morning sickness, my husband threatened to "shake Egg by his bud-like arms." When he began kicking, we called him "Egg Beater."

Finally, a week late, our baby arrived without a lot of fanfare. When my husband held the wizened peanut in his hands for the first time, he looked at me with tears streaming down his face. "Honey, we have Egg," he said proudly.

The obstetrician and nurses in the delivery room all looked at each other oddly, but said nothing. Maybe if we had asked them to put Egg down as our newborn's official name, we would have had more of a reaction, but, strange as it may seem, from that moment on, we never called Timothy "Egg" again.

Part Three

Changes in Longitude and Latitude

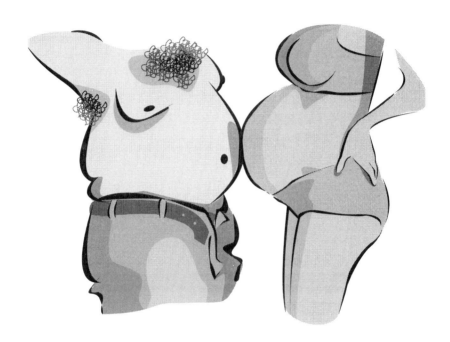

Many of the duds on the racks
made me look like I was wearing
a three-person tent (does that come
in something other than canvas?) or
were far too cute for my liking.

My Boobs Hurt

By Heather Lodge

"My boobs hurt!"

I typed this simple, and perhaps too personal, message and clicked SEND. It was a casual complaint voiced to an old friend, nothing more. Oh, I was puzzled at the pain, but not surprised. After all, I had just stopped taking the birth control pill after nearly ten years, and was expecting a few unpleasant symptoms as my body kicked in and took over its natural cycle again.

"Uh-oh!" Tina's reply came quickly.

Uh-oh? Because my boobs hurt? Before I could type a request for clarification, a second message lit up my screen.

"Did you get your period?"

I thought back. I counted days. I answered, "Well, it's about four days late, but I was pretty irregular before the Pill, so I don't really know when to expect it."

"Go get a test," Tina insisted.

I laughed out loud. Oh sure, my husband and I had discussed trying for our first child together, and although I had stopped taking my prescription a month earlier than we'd originally planned, I figured that we'd have the experience of trying to conceive for at least a few months.

I was determined to maintain a no-pressure attitude. If it happened, great. If not, well, there would always be next month. No big deal.

Several hours and one home pregnancy test later, I was still unconvinced. I e-mailed a digital picture of the urine stick to Tina, logged off, and dialed her number.

"Do you see a line?"

"A what?"

"A line! I don't know if I actually see a line or if I'm just imagining it."

She opened her e-mail and started laughing at me. My spirits fell. Oh, it's not like I actually expected to be pregnant, but the experience of actually taking the test had made me nervous with anticipation nevertheless. "It's negative, isn't it?"

"Um, Heather ... are you looking at the same thing I'm looking at? Because you're pregnant!"

Oh my God! Pregnant? Me? Right away?

I was the statistic-breaker. I was, apparently, fertile. What happened to the trying, to the counting of days and taking of basal metabolic temperatures and lying around postintercourse, afraid of losing a single drop of potential success?

Damn, that was pretty easy.

After a few hours of nervous pacing, I shared the news with my husband and prepared to settle into the acceptance phase. I am pretty predictable. I knew that I'd devour reference books and visit Web sites and gather all of the information necessary to frighten the bejeezus out of myself, the naïve first-timer. I also knew that I wouldn't be able to keep the secret for long. The cautionary voice in my mind suggested that I wait until the end of my first trimester before breaking the news.

I managed to wait a week and a half.

And of course, as soon as the news was out, I was free to do my favorite pre-emptive worrying activity: grilling my been-there friends for the gory details.

Every one of them got the same initial question. It was not about the pain of labor or the many scary-sounding complications that get sensationalized on the half-hour specials on cable. It was not about relaxation techniques or educational toys. It was, quite directly, "So, when are my boobs going to stop hurting?"

This usually met with a shocked stare at first. That's simply not a question for polite company. But even at that early stage, I had given up on politeness in my search for relief. Two tight sportbras, layered, were not enough. If I needed to descend a set of stairs, the only way to do so without shooting pain was to clasp my breasts tightly against my ribcage and move very slowly. Showers were nearly unbearable. My husband spent a few confused yet understanding weeks trying to remember to hug

Changes in Longitude and Latitude

me around the waist instead of the shoulders, and there was one memorable night when I awoke screaming in the wee hours of the morning. Dazed with fear and concern, Joe asked me, "Are you okay?" I had to shamefacedly admit that I'd rolled over in my sleep and bumped one of my tender breasts.

I quickly discovered that while most of the popular guide-books happily discuss medical terminology and the latest trends in parenting, very few of them address the mundane unpleas-antness of pregnancy. The messages that I gathered from most of the media were that pregnancy is a wonderful time during which you glow and revel in your womanhood … or … prepare for bed rest, a lot of medical intervention and an emergency C-section.

There was little middle ground for the normal woman — someone who didn't experience any major problems, but had unexpected and potentially embarrassing complaints. There were entries in the book for everything from insomnia to pre-eclampsia, but nothing beyond "symptoms vary" seemed to address my sore boobs.

Happily, I did find that my more self-assured friends were willing to open up and tell me about some of those icky, nui-sance-type symptoms of pregnancy once they'd gotten over the initial shock of me discussing my boobs in public. I'm glad that I asked, because I learned more in this way than through any other source.

I'm now just past the halfway point of this pregnancy. In a lot of ways, I feel very much older and wiser.

My boobs stopped hurting right on schedule, at the end of my first trimester. Now I bug my friends for advice on heartburn remedies.

I'll probably need those for the next few decades, come to think of it.

Afternoon Sickness

By Cindy Graul

I'd like to clear up one long-standing misconception about morning sickness! For some of us it's: morning, noon and night!

I could tell you even today, every discrete bush, the precise bathroom location in each restaurant, the appropriate places to pull over off the side of the road for a good hurl. And, most of all, the most convenient places for a sudden vomit: showers, bathroom sinks, and kitchen sinks!

Yes, I think I have mastered all locations known to woman, but my all-time favorite story involves the driver's seat.

It was that important day when you must consume the sickeningly sweet orange drink for the diabetes screening test. I was driving from a late morning meeting, drinking the entire bottle on the way to my doctor's. I had to arrive exactly within the hour after consuming it.

Now I had already gotten sick while brushing my teeth that morning and during the middle of my breakfast. On the way into work I pulled over, and once I got to work, while interviewing someone, I had to discretely escort them to the lobby so I could get sick in my trash can. I had already had a full day of the usual routine, although now the pressure was on to make it to the doctor and avoid one more good hurl!

So, I put on the classical FM radio station, cranked up the car AC and slowly drank the drink. Three quarters of the way through, I was feeling great!

WOW!

As I sipped it, my stomach tossed, and tossed, and OHHHH-HHHH my, deep from within, that feeling came over me — the urge to purge this liquid gold.

I sat there mentally talking myself out of it, trying with all my might to tighten my lips shut and return that magic potion back to my belly where it belonged.

But the slimy orange liquid didn't have the same intention.

Changes in Longitude and Latitude

And with one big gush, like Hoover Dam bursting, out flew like a log flume a thunderous explosion, all over my front window and out through my nose! That really burned, let me tell you.

Orange drink slime!!! Yuck!

Now, to make this story worse, I could tell you all the great spots to pull over for moments like this, but this was not one of them! The explosive moment happened in a construction zone, right where you can look at the men taking their snack breaks.

Not a tissue in the car, nor a fast-food napkin. Just my dress to wipe my face and nose and rear view mirror to help me pull what dignity I had left deep inside me.

What Blooming Really Means

By Grace Tierney

Blooming was almost the first pregnancy word I learned, certainly before more intimidating terms such as delivery, labor and natural. As soon as I told anybody I was pregnant, they would get a glazed look, which can only be compared to a farmer at a livestock auction.

They would scan my body for blemishes and bumps, shake their heads slightly and kindly announce, "Congratulations. You're blooming."

I was so intrigued by this term that I looked it up in the dictionary. It is defined as "flourishing, prime, perfection, glowing and a powdery deposit on fruit."

Well, I've heard of sweaty women being described as "glowing" during Victorian times. Certainly the increased level of perspiration was in evidence, but the powdery fruit deposit worried me even more. Surely that means blooming is a polite word for "moldy, rotten and stinky."

I resolved that I would get to the bottom of this blooming business by consulting other mothers. My own was my first port of call. She brought me up to tell it like it is, and she certainly applies the same principle herself. From her perspective, as a trim, good-looking grandmother, she was quite happy to explain that it meant I would be getting fat.

Yes, that's right, no kind words, and no euphemisms, just fat.

After being pulled from her throat in unreasoning pregnant rage (which is only alluded to as "being more sensitive" in the pregnancy books), I decided to join pregnancy yoga and check out the women there who would be further advanced than I was.

I shuffled in, feeling like a strange hormonal stalker because I had no visible proof of my status other than a small stick with a pink line on it. I was horrified to find that they all looked like elephants. All right. So they were elephants that could balance elegantly on one leg while extending their arms above their heads, but they were still scary.

Changes in Longitude and Latitude

Since my main view of them was from a crumpled heap on the floor, I realized that looking at a pregnant woman from that angle has to be one of the bravest things that midwives do.

Things just got worse after that. I found strange, red heat spots on my burgeoning belly. None of my clothes fit anymore, and the mailman lost the maternity outfits I had mail ordered. I kept waiting for my skin and hair to "bloom," but instead they became drier, and when I checked the book, I found the section about the "mask of pregnancy" and panicked.

The father tried to be supportive, but I was too depressed. Reassurances about how lovely I was looking were greeted by derisive snorts. I was too busy glaring at my face in the mirror to heed his kind words. My normally good complexion now resembled that of an evil witch in a fairy tale.

I felt robbed. I mean I had seen all the Hollywood movies where actresses get to look beautiful the whole way through their on-screen pregnancies. They had convinced me that the list of unsightly pregnancy complaints in my book, which included swollen ankles, varicose veins and piles (gulp) was a fabrication of over-anxious medical professionals, but my faith was wavering.

Those medical professionals had already lost my support and I hadn't even experienced labor yet. I spent months carefully watching my diet and exercise before trying for a baby because I knew weight could be an issue. This didn't stop my obstetrician calmly informing me that I was a "shorty" and he warned me in dire terms not to put on too much weight.

Luckily, it was my first visit and I was too awed by seeing my child's sonogram to be able to yell, "Hey, I'm paying you a small fortune to deliver this baby, not to echo my mother! And you're only two inches taller than me anyhow. Even my best friend who is six feet tall doesn't get to call me Shorty!!!"

Was I an unfit mother-in-training because I concentrated on trying to look vaguely attractive despite saggy maternity trousers instead of ordering cots and baby clothes? Why didn't anybody tell me that when you get pregnant you have to abandon all semblance of fashion? The books say "accessorize" for your own style, but honestly, who are they kidding? A nice necklace or scarf is not going to distract attention from that hideously frilly, frumpy sack you're wearing instead of real clothes.

Pink floral tents were the main option available to me. As a long-time stripy-pajama wearer who hates pink with a vengeance, I found out that the only color you can get breast-feeding nightdresses in is, you've guessed it, pink. Usually they're constructed of transparent cotton with some nice nonsensical lace trims.

The only consolation was, at week twenty-two, discovering I had acquired a rather fetching bosom. That was before I tried to buy a nonunderwired support bra in the correct size. My usual lingerie store, which had a wide range of every other possible variety of underwear, stocked just one suitable bra. It looked like something a nun would wear during a pilgrimage and it wasn't even cotton, so it was far from effective for a hot and bothered mother-to-be. No wonder we're "blooming" expectant mothers, we're glowing. Not only that, but I can expect my two frontal friends to get much larger before I will be done with this pregnancy malarkey. I shall have to locate a tent-making factory for my next fitting.

Desperate for a compliment, I wore a cleavage-revealing top over my nun-bra last weekend for my birthday dinner with girl-friends. They were all so busy getting mellow on the wine that I couldn't drink that not one of them noticed my lovely upper body.

"Thou shalt not be a sexy mama" must be engraved over the maternity-ward doors.

All of them spotted the bump and commented on that instead. Obviously, when you're pregnant, that is all you can be, a bump with a woman attached as an afterthought. Now that I think of it, that's the answer.

Blooming means: "Beware of the woman with bump."

Kegal-Woman

By Kirsten Hines

"You know, when you are peeing, you stop peeing in mid-stream."

I looked in bewilderment at my friend. "What?" I replied.

"They are called kegal exercises. They are necessary when you are pregnant, so you don't pee yourself when you sneeze or laugh really hard."

I had read all the books on pregnancy and thought some things must be exaggerated. My girlfriend and I were sitting at lunch, she pregnant with her third baby, me with my first. I was trying to clear up all the myths of pregnancy. Surely, this must be one. My mother had never told me she had loss of bladder control. But, then again, she never told me anything about pregnancy.

I woke up every day after that — and did them every hour on the hour, sometimes while peeing, other times at my desk while I was working.

I snickered to myself. No one knew I was exercising my kegal muscle.

I gave birth to my first child, a beautiful little boy by cae-sarean section. The icing on the cake, I could sneeze, laugh and jump for joy, and did not pee on myself. I was the champion grand master kegal-woman.

Two years later, I was bragging to another friend, pregnant with her first, me with my second, telling her how she must do her kegal exercises regularly, or else she will succumb to the shameful self-peeing. I instructed her to do exactly as I did so she, too, would be successful.

Two months later we were out to lunch again, allergy season had started, and I couldn't stop sneezing.

One ... two ... three ... "Uh-oh."

My girlfriend looked at me and said, "What? Are you having

contractions? Are you okay?"

I looked up at her, with tears in my eyes, "No, I peed myself!!"

I couldn't believe it, I was no longer the grand master. I was doing my exercises the same as during the first pregnancy. What could have happened?

After talking with friends who have gone through several pregnancies, I learned that the kegal exercises didn't work for them either. They had all thought they were doing everything correctly: kegal exercises daily, hourly, every time they had a chance.

Apparently, it doesn't matter.

So whenever you see a woman with a child who sneezes, don't just say "bless you."

She needs so much more than that.

The Skinny on Pregnancy

By Cheryl Fury

Like so many of my friends, I delayed procreation until my thirties. I was too busy amassing university degrees and enjoying myself in my twenties. Two sons later, a solo trip to the bathroom now qualifies as "quality time" by myself, and a rare excursion to a restaurant without a clown and a drive-through is equated with "fine-dining." Therefore, I am glad I made the most of my life B.C. (before children) when I had to worry only about wiping my own nose and cutting my own meat.

Certainly my husband and I were excited to embark on the wild ride that is parenting; after an inauspicious beginning — urinating on a stick while trying to miss my hand — we hit the home pregnancy-test jackpot. There is inexplicable Darwinian pride about passing on your DNA and joining the not-so-exclusive club of Breeders. But after crossing the parental Rubicon, there is no more time to contemplate whether we should have had a trial run with a puppy.

In the first trimester, I looked for signs that I was really expecting. I found them in not so subtle ways. My breasts were so sore that a bra felt like a medieval torture device. I was exhausted by the mere THOUGHT of walking across the room, but somehow I willed myself through each day, daydreaming about falling asleep with a crashing thud by 7 p.m. I was subjected to hot flashes so severe I had no use for heat in the car during an entire winter in the Great White North.

Yet, I managed to dodge the morning sickness bullet and hemorrhoids.

Through close friends I got to experience them vicariously. One pregnant friend threatened to burn off her hemorrhoids with a lighter if she wasn't taken to the Emergency Room for immediate de-roiding. Another beached her naked carcass spread eagle in front of a fan to quell the burning ring of fire.

Besides the moral support, friends are essential. They lend

you maternity clothes. This saves you from taking out a second mortgage in order to finance your "expectant" wardrobe. Finding appropriate clothes for the workplace was the greatest challenge. Many of the duds on the racks made me look like I was wearing a three-person tent (does that come in something other than canvas?) or were far too cute for my liking. One can not feel empowered in a meeting with teddy bears on your blouse.

Leisure wear was easier to procure. I resorted to poaching my husband's clothes. I knew when his 2XL T-shirts got too tight around the middle that it was time to give birth, go naked or Scarlet O'Hara the bedspread into a maternity frock for the homestretch. I now understood why Victorian women went into "confinement" during that latter part of their pregnancies: Their whale-bone corsets had blown their staves long before and they were far too large and cranky to be fit company in respectable society.

Panties were a particular annoyance in the last weeks, but I couldn't bring myself to shell out the cash for maternity under-wear. In desperation, I stole my husband's biggest, baggiest box-ers. By the final weeks, I dispensed with underwear altogether whenever possible. I hadn't seen my nether regions for months, and it was only the constant urination that reminded me I had working parts down there at all.

I did, of course, wear proper undergarments for my frequent visits to the ob-gyn. I'm not sure why I maintained such formali-ties since my ob-gyn had no compunction about keeping instruments that looked like something out of *Dead Ringers*™ in a bucket at the foot of the examination table. By the end of those forty long weeks of pregnancy, I had my feet in stirrups so often I could have qualified for any equestrian event.

Many of these specialists are in high demand and there is a veritable parade of pregos waddling into their offices, waiting to be weighed and probed. Experience tells me that the best ob-gyns are those who have actually pushed something eight pounds or larger through a ten-centimeter orifice in their body. If they haven't, no amount of observation or academic knowledge allows them to "get it," particularly if they have a penis.

Choose an ob-gyn who doesn't make you wait for extended

periods of time, especially if there is only one bathroom (which is usually located down a distant corridor). If they only knew how much hormone-driven crankiness was bubbling —barely — below the surface, there would be an express lane in the doctor's office based on due date. "Going postal" pales by comparison to a prego packing an extra forty pounds and a bad attitude.

For the most part, I enjoyed my pregnancies except for those final weeks. The end of the last trimester, like prison time, is slow time.

Sleep, too, seemed to be a thing of the past. This is Providence's way of preparing you for those sleepless nights to come. The struggle to obtain a minimum level of comfort was challenging enough, but this was complicated by Junior's nocturnal tango. Regardless of how much your partner wants to share the experience of carrying your child, these dances are only for two — and Baby always leads.

Robbed of the simple joy of sleep and culinary delights, one obsesses about evicting the lodger. I tried almost every home remedy to bring on labor — pizza, rides on bumpy roads, castor oil — but nothing worked. I didn't resort to sex — I figured I wouldn't throw my body at an ugly blind man let alone a sighted one like my husband, especially since I was wearing his briefs.

I did contemplate using a knitting needle to see if I could break my own water, but opted for yet another ride in a Jeep with shoddy suspension. A high degree of discomfort is nature's way of making the mother want to get a large baby out a little door.

I never considered it a problem that I chose a mate two feet taller and a hundred pounds heavier than me. Although carrying his sons didn't do me in, getting them out was a completely different matter. (Hat size is worth noting when you're dating.) Therefore, I had no reservations about drugs during labor.

There are no Purple Hearts for natural childbirth, and as a mother of two rough and tumble boys who think diaper changing is a contact sport, there is plenty of pain afterward when an epidural is not available. My strategy was to wait until I got far enough along in my labor that I welcomed the idea of a really big needle in my spine. The possibility of paralysis seemed inviting rather than a liability.

Where do I sign?

Whoever said you forget about the pain of childbirth clearly never experienced it. As miraculous as the experience is, I must admit I made a number of very pointed comments about design flaws that I then stuffed in God's suggestion box. However, when you hold your very own wrinkly bundle with a cone head and your eyes, every tear, 'roid and stretchmark seems like a battle wound — a very acceptable price of a great victory.

My Milk-Depot Years

By S. (Shae) A. Cooke

All of the girls in my family have flat chests, including me. My twin brother is the only family member to sport one of measurable size — he has a pigeon chest.

He detests it. I covet it.

My husband tells me he fell in love with the "inner me," and that breast size doesn't matter. Hello? A woman of even moderate proportion walks by in a spaghetti strap and his head does a Linda-Blaire-in-the-Exorcist 360-degree-turn. He loses his hearing and his voice, but his farsightedness seems to improve.

Limited Time Offer

One day, soon after my cousin got a secret boob job, we had a family reunion. In my sister's room, she took off her shirt and said, "I've been taking these bust developing pills — check these out!" With wonder, we wrote down the name of the product, each pouncing for the bottle. My cousin laughed so hard until it dawned on us what she had done. We inspected her hooters as one would a new vehicle, asking about the model, searching for scratch marks or dents and wondering about warranty.

Hot Little Number

Enter motherhood — my milk-depot years. My husband's spaghetti-strap fantasies came true. Cleavage became a household word. My gnat bites, err ... breasts grew to unbelievable proportions. At first, I planned to breastfeed only for the first six months, but my husband encouraged me to continue longer. When my breasts were engorged, he'd get a crazed, far-away look and say, "Get a sitter, put on that saucy red number, we're going out on the town."

Las Vegas or Bust.

Before the baby, I worried that my small bust size would affect my milk supply. No problem. My little milkman had a voracious appetite. The more he drank, the more I produced, and he liked only my brand. There was no way he was going to settle for latex or rubber nipples. I produced enough milk to feed the neighborhood. My boobs got bigger and bigger. I was in double-D heaven. It was nice finally having mine noticed and appreciated.

My euphoria was short lived. It just wasn't acceptable to breastfeed my son until I sent him off to college, no matter how much my husband begged … err … wanted me to.

Land Ho!

Don't believe the doctors and lactation experts when they tell you that there are no ill effects to your breasts, postbreast-feeding. Many insisted that I would retain some of the extra fat and enjoy an added cup size when I stopped. My women friends were much less optimistic and advised that they were more likely to deflate and point south. Last time I looked, they were on a southeasterly course.

Flash Fiction

If there is one thing I've learned through all this, it is this: Even if a man insists that he is a leg man, don't believe it. As surely as a bear poops in the woods, the truth will surface — either in the lingerie department of Sears, while watching *Baywatch*™ reruns or in motherhood years.

A Visit from the Titty Fairy

By Kirsten Hines

I think we have all heard of the Titty Fairy, and the magic that she brings to women all around the world who never had breasts until they gave birth.

I was one of those women. I was a 34A before I gave birth to my son, but then the Titty Fairy visited me. When I started nursing I was a whopping 38DD.

I couldn't believe it.

I would look in the mirror and say to myself, "So, this is what it is like to have breasts!"

My husband was in heaven, prancing like a peacock next to his wife, now with her glorious 38DD. It didn't matter that my figure hadn't come back 100 percent, because now, I had breasts!!

I was a voluptuous woman.

I could no longer fit into any of my clothing, so it was time to go shopping! A whole new wardrobe was needed.

Shopping was a nightmare. I am a very petite woman and, well, they just don't make clothes for someone who is a size six and a 38DD. Every top I put on was pulling at the seams. I just couldn't find anything to fit me. I ended up buying shirts two sizes too big. Instead of being this voluptuous woman, I now looked frumpy.

I knew the solution, it was time to start exercising again! It had been six weeks since I had given birth, so my doctor gave me the go-ahead. I went to the gym and jumped on the treadmill and started running. My glorious 38DD certainly did not like that; I don't know how those *Baywatch*™ Babes did it with smiles on their faces while running down the beach.

My breasts were bouncing up, then down, then sideways — and it was painful! How was I supposed to get back into shape with these things? The Titty Fairy sure did a number on me! I couldn't fit into my clothes, couldn't exercise, but, yes, my breasts looked good naked.

After a few months, my 38DD finally settled down, and sagged.

So to all those flat-chested women out there, be careful what you wish for. The Titty Fairy may grant it!

Confessions of a Seatbelt Zealot

By Christine Allen-Riley

I'd like to tell you that I had the kind of pregnancy of which soon-to-be new mothers dream:

- The one where you look as good as Demi Moore on the cover of *Vanity Fair*.

- The one where you exude a soft, radiant glow and your Zen-like sense of calm never wavers.

- The one where you actually enjoy being pregnant.

Yes, I'd like to tell you that I had that pregnancy, but I'd be lying more than my mother when she said, "You'll forget about the pain as soon as you hold your baby."

Yeah, right.

By the time I reached my ninth month, I thought I'd had my quota of pregnancy mishaps. I thought perhaps I could just relax for the last couple of weeks. That may have been my biggest mistake.

My husband was out of town on business with our one-and-only car, so I had to borrow my little brother's car in order to make it to my doctor's appointment. Like the automobiles of many eighteen-year-olds, Martin's car (a baby blue, eighty-something Ford Tempo) was crammed full of sticky soda bottles, rancid fast food wrappers and empty cigarette packages. A sour stench emanated from the upholstery. Trying not to lose my lunch, I cleared a spot, shut the ashtray and gingerly wedged myself behind the wheel. That's when I remembered the missing driver's-side window. Instead of glass, the car sported a stunning combination of mostly clear sheet plastic and duct tape.

Sadly, it was February.

In Michigan.

During a blizzard.

I moved the seat forward. In order to reach the pedals, I had to rest my giant, nearly-ready-to-give-birth-belly in the steering wheel. Ignominious, but necessary. Being the seatbelt zealot I am, I fastened the restraint as soon as I got situated.

The drive to the doctor's office was fairly uneventful, despite having to peel back the plastic window to check for oncoming traffic. I even got the last spot in the frozen, ice-covered parking lot.

And then my luck ran out.

I hit the release on the seatbelt clasp. It didn't budge. I tried again. Nothing. With a sinking feeling, I realized I had to pee. I tried not to panic. It didn't work. In a fit of misguided optimism, I thought perhaps I could wiggle out of the restraint.

Take the journey with me, people. Nine months pregnant with my second child. Giant belly shoved in the steering wheel well. Bound to a smelly, garbage-filled excuse for a car, attempting to shimmy out of a securely latched seatbelt. Did I mention the part about having to pee?

Spotting a screwdriver on the passenger-side floor, I kicked off a shoe and sock. Somehow, I managed to pick it up with my toes. I tried to jimmy the latch open and succeeded only in breaking the screwdriver.

By this time, my baby happily bounced on my bladder like a demented circus clown. I knew, unless something drastic happened soon, I'd add another unfortunate smell to my brother's car.

Five long, long minutes later, I was ready to cry. And then I saw her. An angel. The patron saint of nearly hysterical pregnant women everywhere. The only sign of life in the parking lot since I'd pulled up.

Any dignity I might have possessed was long gone. I yelled for help. Okay, I admit, it was more of a shriek. A tall, lovely woman in a full-length fur coat opened the passenger side door. Perfectly coifed and dripping in diamonds, she scanned the interior. Her expensive perfume wafted in and clashed with the foul stench of the traveling landfill. Her delicate, and likely costly, nose wrinkled.

I tried to explain my dilemma. Only, what popped out of my mouth was, "It's not my car. Really." She appeared understandably puzzled, so I launched into the sad story of my dismal condition. She smiled and assured me she'd be right back. Within moments, she returned with a pair of office scissors and cut me free. I squirmed from the car, barely noticing the steering wheel shaped ring of grime around my belly.

Then my savior turned on me. She asked me to return the shears to the receptionist at my doctor's office. Once inside, I traded the scissors for a sample cup and ducked into the bathroom for the most gratifying urinating experience of my life.

When I exited the restroom, the office staff averted their eyes and stifled giggles. The nurse who took me to be weighed actually held the clipboard in front of her face. As I passed the lab area, the techs snickered and pointed. For once, I was glad to get to the exam room and strip. I hoped I didn't smell like Martin's car.

Figuring my ordeal was over I tried to read. All they had in the room were those baby magazines with air-brushed photos of new mothers in the throes of blissful maternity. The ones designed to make the average woman weep with the injustice of it all. I was interrupted by rapid whispers and muffled laughter outside the door. To her credit, my doctor attempted to keep a straight face when she entered the exam room. It lasted all of fifteen seconds. Having heard my saga, she asked permission to share the story with some of her other patients. She thought it would help cheer the depressed ones.

Little did I know my doctor would find it so amusing, she'd keep telling the story for six years. A few months ago, I ran into a friend who was feeling overwhelmed by her pregnancy. She told me our doctor had just shared my tale of woe at her latest appointment.

Yup, that's me.

I'm the poster girl for weak-bladdered women everywhere.

So remember, always wear your seatbelt — unless, of course, you're hugely pregnant, very nearly incontinent and driving your little brother's car.

Big Mama Underpants

By Margaret Yang

As everyone knows, pregnancy is divided into trimesters. All the medical books and even my best girlfriends told me that certain things were supposed to happen at certain times. Never mind that I was still nauseated in months four and five. Never mind that I was nowhere near "glowing" until the baby was ready to pop. Never mind that the increased sex drive in the second trimester passed me by completely.

So there I was, cruising into my seventh month, feeling pretty darned good, even though I wasn't supposed to. Everyone said the third trimester was the worst, consisting of insomnia, backache and endless heartburn, none of which described me. Was I just fooling myself? Was I in for a tremendous letdown?

Passage from trimesters one to two happened gradually: each day a little less queasy, each day a little less svelte. Passage into the third trimester happened in about three minutes. Boom! Suddenly I went from cutely pregnant to BIG MAMA.

It happened in the underwear department.

I'd been getting by with my usual cotton bikini underwear in a larger size than usual, which come in a rainbow of attractive colors. They fit nicely under my little bump of a belly, and even when I was dressing and undressing, I wasn't appalled by my figure in the bathroom mirror. I thought the look was cute, and (dare I say it?) even a little sexy.

Until last Saturday, when the elastic in my faithful bikini undies started cutting off the circulation in my legs. I had no choice. It was time for the dreaded maternity underwear.

So, I went to the store, where they had three classes of undergarments: I-wanna-feel-sexy lace, practical cotton and ugly maternity. I headed for ugly maternity. Let's see ... size small fits hips from 32 to 50 inches. I don't know a pregnant woman alive who has hips 32 inches! Size medium fits hips 50 to 62 inches. Yeah, that sounded more like my bubble butt. I got two packs of mediums, in hopelessly dowdy shades of pink and yellow and

Changes in Longitude and Latitude

blue. Got them home, tried them on ...

And instantly lost my self-esteem.

These things are huge! They cover my entire belly, with the top ending about an inch below my bra line. In fact, I could tuck them under my bra and make my own "onesie." And they have legs cut like those boy-leg swimsuits. These are the kind of underpants I wore when I was six. These are the kind of underpants my mother wears. And my grandmother. These are the kind of underpants my husband calls "army issue combat undies."

The only problem is ... they're comfortable.

Part Four

I Think Therefore I …
What?

*Physical thickness I had anticipated,
but becoming the intellectual equal
of a golden retriever came as a
not-very-welcome surprise.*

Confessions of a Knocked-Up Knucklehead

By Anita Kugelstadt

About four months into my first pregnancy, a friend of mine who was already a mother sent me a care package. In it, among other things, was a bottle of rum with instructions attached. "Dad-to-be: drink this when mom-to-be is having her mood swings." I had snorted derisively. The idea was ludicrous. Mood swings were for the weak of mind.

Twenty minutes of inexplicable sobbing at the supper table that same night convinced me that mood swings might be a fundamental part of life for some months to come. So would leg cramps, headaches and backache.

Pregnancy two added hemorrhoids, breathlessness, exhaustion and dizziness to my inventory of life experiences.

Pregnancy three offered nausea, constipation, heartburn, burst capillaries and hips so loose that I had to call people from other rooms to move my legs for me.

Oh yes, I recall a yeast infection. Stretchmarks arrived early and stayed late. Okay, they never really left. But none of this is particularly notable. Many women could take my list and raise me bleeding gums and varicose veins.

What is notable then?

How about a symptom not listed in any mother-and-baby-care book I read? A side effect left unmentioned by all of my health-care providers, yet common to each of my pregnancies. Without a doubt it's the darkest secret signature of motherhood. There is, of course, no medical term, so how shall I say this?

Enhanced stupefaction.

Augmented doltishness.

Improved thickness.

And I don't mean my waist, or even my ankles. Physical thickness I had anticipated, but becoming the intellectual equal of a golden retriever came as a not-very-welcome surprise.

Of course, my imbecility did not arrive as a bolt from the blue. I even managed to finish my thesis during the initial months of my first pregnancy. But intellect was leaking away, steadily, and by my third pregnancy, that trickle had become a torrent.

Let's say that before my first pregnancy I was fairly well respected as an intelligent being (I won't insist this is true. I'm just saying let's pretend for the sake of clarification). By month nine I had slumped to the level of a dolphin. Delivery returned me to normalcy, but from the moment I conceived my second child, I plummeted without delay back down to the dolphin and degraded from there to retriever. Pregnancy three knocked me right out of the mammalian class and left me operating around the level of a chicken.

In fact, conceiving my third child dulled my wits so quickly that it took me close to three months to figure out I was pregnant — I thought I had the flu. My "flu" left me unable to do anything more challenging than clean the house, and so I used my time to organize the basement and then gave away most of the baby articles I had stored there.

By the end of my third pregnancy, my beleaguered gray matter didn't even rate chicken level. I confess I was closer to a goldfish, which is no small coincidence, since a pregnant goldfish is known as a twit. How is it that a goldfish rates a special name when she is with fry, yet a woman with child is simply a pregnant woman? Goldfish/twit, I'm afraid, will be my starting point if I have a fourth child.

A sobering thought.

The effects of my simplemindedness were many. I remember complaining bitterly about the holes in my socks and how manufacturers couldn't even fabricate socks. My partner looked at me in a queer sort of way for the six, maybe seven hundredth time that day. "You don't have holes in your socks," he offered. Before I could access the glacier in my head for a sufficiently cutting response, he continued, "I mean, they're not your socks."

I Think Therefore I … What?

I looked down at my feet. The tops of my socks barely reached my ankle bones. The fabric stretched so thin I appeared to be wearing threads, except where six of my toes stuck out (not on the same foot I assure you). I was wearing my daughter's socks. My four-year-old daughter's socks.

I became a riotous source of amusement for my children. One night during supper, I foolishly attempted to multitask, a skill I normally possess in spades. Instead of concentrating solely on making my fajita, I endeavored to simultaneously engage in conversation. The result? I grabbed the bowl full of fajita ingredients and cheerfully filled it with milk, leaving me holding what appeared to be a bowl of cereal for a giant, if cereal were made of red peppers, onions and chicken.

Nor was my husband disappointed by my dim-wittedness. For one thing, I could no longer accuse him of not remembering what I told him, mainly because I couldn't remember what I'd told him either. Or what I wanted to tell him for that matter.

Furthermore, having conversations like, "Honey, what do you call those rectangle things we build houses out of …?"

"You mean bricks?" gave him a sense of intellectual and verbal superiority that he enjoyed.

Surely other women spend hours of their pregnancies ambling from room to room in their homes, furrowing their brows and looking for clues to their intentions, lose the capacity to speak their mother tongue with proficiency or try to send their kids to school on a Saturday.

Stupidity, like misery, loves company, so why hasn't this temporary but very real affliction rated even a mention, let alone its own talk show?

Well, absolutely no need to stay silent in shame. Sure, stupid isn't pretty, but if I may be so brazen, perhaps my being a nincompoop served an evolutionary purpose: a well-developed ability to forget makes having more than one child a possibility. I guess I was just sheer dumb lucky.

I've decided to prepare name tags for the whole family, in the event we decide on a fourth child.

The Pen

By Kate M. Jackson

At eight months pregnant, I was writing thank-you notes for my baby shower, when I lost my favorite pen. I got up to answer the phone, but when I returned to my task, my pen had mysteriously disappeared.

I glanced around my disheveled desk, looking beneath the scatter of papers and empty coffee cups — no pen. I looked on the floor, under the desk and even retraced my steps to the phone and back — still, no pen. I figured my pug, Vito, was up to his usual tomfoolery, so I checked under the couch where he often hoarded his stolen goods. I found a navy blue sock, a throw pillow, a few used fabric softener sheets and my hairdryer.

But no pen.

I chalked it up to pregnancy mindlessness and abandoned my thank-you notes in favor of prebaby errands. The remainder of the afternoon, I did some grocery shopping, went to the dentist and met a friend for a manicure and a pedicure.

When I returned home, I transferred my bundles to one hand, climbed the stairs and reached up to turn my key. Suddenly, I felt something roll along my belly, hit my shoe and tumble onto the doorstep.

My pen, sweaty and linty, stared back at me.

Apparently, it had been cowering beneath my left breast all day long. My breasts, which had become as large and hard as candlepin bowling balls, had evidently copped a vice-like grip on my pen when I had gotten up to answer the phone.

After a mini re-creation, I discovered the pen had actually been lodged between my boobs and belly as if stuck between two couch cushions. I no longer had breasts (plural), I had a bosom (singular).

For those unfamiliar with the bosom, let me elaborate: A bosom is a single boob that hangs like a sausage-shaped shelf across the chest.

It is most common in nuns, great aunts and schoolteachers

over the age of seventy.

My elation at finding the pen quickly turned to panic as I mentally retraced my steps that day, remembering the odd looks I'd received. I'd caught the manicurist tossing a few sideways glances at me, but my friend swore she just had a lazy eye. I had caught the cashier in the grocery store staring at my chest, but I, feeling self-loathing, hormonal and bloated, was not offended but pleased to receive the attention.

Thinking back, my dentist had to have seen the pen peeking out, but I guess pointing out a pen jammed under one's bosom isn't quite the same as informing someone that she has spinach in her teeth.

Once again, I was experiencing the mania of pregnancy. A side effect of sharing your body and brain cells with your developing baby, this pregnancy mania comes from a restless energy within you that often bubbles over, pushing aside logic and reason.

I became so absentminded and flaky that I could have lost a game of checkers to my pug.

I know my husband probably wondered what happened to the somewhat coherent woman he had married. But this had to take the cake: I was trying to see what the load capacity was under my bosom and had already learned I could hold a magic marker, a flip-flop and a packet of Fig Newtons. He walked into the kitchen and found me holding a spatula beneath my breasts.

At eight months into the mania, there was nothing left to do but laugh.

Evening Shoes

By Lisa Nicholl

At twenty-six weeks my membranes ruptured. I was confined to my hospital bed. There I lay for seven weeks with nothing to do but watch my favorite TV shows, read trashy romance novels and fulfill my cravings, which, at the time, was anything over 500 calories per mouthful.

You can only imagine how much weight one can gain from these practices; however, it was what I needed to do to keep myself sane and my unborn child inside me for as long as possible.

At least that is how I justified the extra fifty pounds I gained while I was there.

But I digress. My stay was as pleasant as one could expect. The nurses were superb, my ob-gyn was also a friend who made sure that my semi-private room remained private for the most part. I had no complaints really. The only thing I was really missing was contact with the outside world. The people who worked everyday, went to parties, movies and out for dinner … how I longed to joined them if only for a night.

You can imagine my excitement when my doctor told me I won a get-out-of-jail-free card. This would allow me to leave the hospital grounds for four hours. Four whole hours! Whatever would I do with myself.

The words were barely out of my doctor's mouth and I was on the phone to my husband to come and get me. Quick!

Immediately I went to my closet-suitcase to find something to wear. I chose one of the three maternity outfits I had left that fit. I washed my hair and put makeup on, which seemed to take longer to apply. Was I out of practice? Was my face three times its normal size so there was more to cover?

I was ready to go for my night on the town.

The drive that normally took my husband twenty minutes seemed to take hours. Where could he be? Did he not know how important this was to me? After pacing the halls, I decided to wait by the elevator, that way we wouldn't waste precious minutes walking anymore than we had to.

Finally he arrived. I was ready to pounce on him.

"Where have you been ...? Do you know how long I have been waiting ...?"

I decided to refrain. I did not want to do anything to jeopardize this night. After all, he held the keys to my freedom. Without him, I am back in room 203 deciding whether to have the Salisbury steak with pretend sear marks or the chicken à la king — a disgusting example of what not to do with leftovers.

No, instead I kissed him hello and darted into the elevator. The walk to the car was liberating; I was breathing fresh air. Well, it was Hamilton, but I'd take it over stale hospital air any day.

It was late November and cold. We had just received our first snowfall of the season. I longed to touch the snow and hear the crunch under my feet as we walked. The snow was cold on my feet, colder than I remembered it to be. Had it been that long since I had been outside. Oh well. I mustn't complain. Who knows when I will feel it again?

On the way to the restaurant, I could not help but notice how many people were out and about, driving in their cars, walking down the streets, taking in the newly hung holiday decorations.

I had watched these people through the window of room 203 for what felt like an eternity. I had longed to be like them, and tonight I was. Tonight I was just another pregnant woman out for dinner with her husband.

We entered the restaurant and were seated immediately ahead of others who had been waiting. They graciously allowed me to go ahead of them once they saw my protrusion.

I loved it.

I missed all the privileges one receives being pregnant. When my husband and I were seated, I barely said two words to him, I was completely engrossed in the menu. My selection was very important.

Yes, selections.

After all, I was eating for two, you know. While my husband looked over the wine list, which I couldn't partake in, I decided to venture over to the dessert bar. That way I will have enough time to deliberate my selection during dinner.

As I walked through the restaurant, my feet still freezing from the snow, I couldn't help but notice people looking at me. They seemed to be staring at my legs or my feet. I couldn't quite tell. I looked down but of course with the addition to my stomach, I could not see beyond my belly button.

I shrugged it off. Maybe I was just being paranoid because it was the first time I had been out in public for so long. Or perhaps I was glowing. I decided to ask my husband if he noticed anything when I return. Of course, I was so excited about my dessert choices I forgot to ask.

Naturally, I had to use the washroom right before my meal arrived. I made my way to the washroom, but not without more people staring at my legs/feet. I only knew that both were still there because my stomach was still four feet above the ground when I was vertical. I vowed again to remember to ask my hubby if he noticed anything.

In the washroom, I unloaded all the paraphernalia I was given by the hospital: antiseptic wipes for the toilet seat to prevent my unborn child being at the mercy of somebody else's germs, perinatal squeeze bottle to prevent my unborn child being at risk to MY germs.

Finally I could sit down. The moment I sat down I was in absolute horror.

Beyond my very large maternity pants were two big red pompoms.

No. It can't be. Surely I didn't? I pulled my pants back so that I could see what everyone had been staring at.

My slippers!

I had been in the hospital for so long that I had forgotten to wear shoes!

Part Five

Let the Professionals
Do the Job

*Twenty-six hours into that
experience, and a couple of minutes
after I told the obstetrician,
"YOU push, Buddy!" it finally
occurred to me that death was not
tapping me on the shoulder anytime
soon — or at least not soon enough
to get me out of this mess.*

The Toes Are Supposed to Be There, Doctor

By Tami Crea

I was a nervous first-time mother with a family doctor instead of an ob-gyn. My gentle, soft-spoken doctor assured me that sonograms could be dangerous, and since my pregnancy was proceeding normally, one was not necessary.

Not knowing any better, I believed him.

At eight months, he was doing a manual exam when a very concerned look crossed his face.

He sat back and said very carefully, "I don't want to alarm you, but I think I feel a mass on the baby's head. We need to schedule a sonogram."

With that, he wrote instructions on a piece of paper and ushered me out the door. I waited in agony for the appointment the next day.

When I walked in, the technician informed me that she would not be able to tell me the results of the sonogram and that I should be sure to schedule a follow-up with my doctor. (As if I wasn't already so freaked out, I would just ignore this!)

She gooped up my swollen belly and started swooshing around. Suddenly, she started to laugh. By this time, my already frayed nerves snapped.

"What could possibly be so funny?" I yelled.

She apologized, wiped her eyes and said, "Your baby is just fine. He's just upside down with one leg down in the birth canal. What the doctor was feeling wasn't a mass on the head — it was toes!"

After a scheduled C-section, my beautiful (and perfect) little boy and I went home.

Needless to say, when I got pregnant with my second child, I did NOT go back to that doctor.

This Ain't My First Time Around, Doc

By Candy Killion

The first time I had a baby, I thought I was going to die.

Twenty-six hours into that experience, and a couple of minutes after I told the obstetrician, "YOU push, Buddy!" it finally occurred to me that death was not tapping me on the shoulder anytime soon — or at least not soon enough to get me out of this mess.

There were lots of little informational tidbits they just glossed over in Lamaze class. Like this being a training hospital — a virtual megaplex of greenhorn interns and nursing students — meant that laboring mothers would randomly be asked permission to allow in a small trainee audience to view the action.

By the time my first labor had successfully ended, I had been the spotlight star for "Eight Nurses Between My Legs for the Shave," better known as "Hey, Watch the Razor Down There. I Need That Part Later!" and "How Many Doctors Does It Take for One Little Episiotomy?"

You get my drift. By the time, three-and-a-half years later, I was rolled into the labor room for the second round at center stage, I was jaded. I was seasoned. I was in no mood for training anybody.

Enter Dr. Has-learned-just-enuf-to-be-arrogant. "How are we feeling today?"

"Unless you have a uterus and feel like your spine is being torn out with a rake, I think you need to drop the 'we' stuff, Doc."

Unflappable, Dr. H. presses on. "Have we had our enema?"

"I've had mine."

"Good, good. I see we are at eight centimeters. It's still a little while longer."

"Great. Unhook me from all the bells and whistles for a couple of seconds. I need to make one more trip to the bathroom."

Let the Professionals Do the Job

"Oh, that's impossible. We've had our enema already. What we are feeling is the pressure of the baby in the birth canal."

"Uh ... excuse me? We are feeling the need to hit the toilet."

"I told you, Ma'am. Perhaps you didn't understand me. Let me explain that again. It is perfectly common for us to be feeling more pressure as the baby makes its way down our birth canal."

"Listen, Pal. You are not sailing down my canal. What is happening here is that I really — and I mean, really — must use the bathroom. Now."

"We won't do that. It really isn't necessary. If the sensation is that strong, push. Push. That's what we are supposed to do."

By now, Dr. H. had also assembled a small army of nursing students behind him in a semicircle. From the smirks and eye-rolling going on behind his back, it was obvious that his holier-than-thou routine was already into reruns.

I took a deep breath, and I pushed until I could feel the veins in my neck distend. No baby yet, but I delivered more than I bargained for.

The students roared.

One even applauded.

Dr. H. vomited on his shoes.

I don't think he went anywhere near obstetrics and gynecology after that — and, certainly not internal medicine.

All in all, "we" had quite a learning experience.

I'm Not Too Old!

By Jan Andersen

When I discovered, at the tender age of thirty-nine, that I was pregnant for the fourth time, I was horrified to find myself being referred to as a geriatric mother who, by the time my child had reached school age, would have a brain like puréed baby food and the personality of a stuffed parrot. Despite my advancing years and all the grim statistics about declining fertility, I had conceived after the first time trying with my partner, Mike, who is twelve years my junior.

My three other children from my first marriage had been conceived when I was barely twenty-something, at a time when I was still regarded as a normal, young mother with all her faculties intact. This time, I was led to believe that I would probably forget where I'd left my baby.

I immediately began scouring the Internet for articles and statistics on pregnancy over forty, since that was the age I would be at the time of the birth, and I began to panic. Terms like chromosomal defects, fetal abnormalities, miscarriage, diabetes, placental abruption, pre-eclampsia, placenta previa, prolapse (of everything) and stillbirth leapt out of the page at me.

I soon became convinced that if I didn't miscarry within the first twelve weeks, I would go on to develop every pregnancy complication in the book. Even if I did succeed in producing a full-term, healthy baby, apparently my tortured pelvic muscles would cause everything to collapse and my bladder and reproductive organs would dangle precariously between my legs forevermore, not to mention my breasts, which would probably metamorphose into two flaps of skin like a spaniel's ears.

Eleven weeks into my much-welcome pregnancy, I met with my midwife for the first time. "Ooh, an older mom," was the first thing she said, followed by a non-too-reassuring chortle, as she began filling out the reams of documentation and noted my date of birth. "You don't look that old," she said, apparently trying to make me feel better.

Let the Professionals Do the Job

"I'm in my forties," she continued, "and knowing what I know, I'd never have the courage to have another one at my age," she said, snorting loudly, with her ample chest vibrating in synchronization with each peal of laughter.

After completing all the relevant forms, a process through which the midwife merrily cracked insensitive jokes about pre-historic mothers, she took my blood pressure and checked for the baby's heartbeat.

At each antenatal appointment, my blood pressure was comfortably low, my uterus was exactly the right size for dates, the baby's heartbeat was strong and my pregnancy was progressing normally. However, each time a particular symptom was revealed, such as pelvic discomfort or backache, my midwife immediately attributed it to my age with clichés such as, "Well, you're not getting any younger you know."

At twelve weeks, I met my obstetric consultant for the first time. It was the first of several appointments where I would have to exercise dexterity in urinating into a two-inch-diameter plastic cup without dribbling all over my hands.

When we were finally ushered into the consultant's room, he immediately launched into a bulletin of depressing statistics on the chances of a woman over thirty-five conceiving a child with some degree of chromosomal abnormality. He also talked about the increased risks of miscarriage, pre-eclampsia, preterm labor and multiple births.

I felt like saying, "And will you be managing my labor with one of those hoists that you attach to elderly people when lifting them out of the bath?"

Following the pessimistic views of the consultant, I opted for amniocentesis, so a date for the procedure was, therefore, duly booked for June 10, 1999, four days after my fortieth birthday.

Two days before we received the results, I had a routine antenatal appointment with my jovial midwife. "No news is good news," she chortled, after I'd expressed my anxiety at not having yet heard anything.

"You've asked to know the sex too, haven't you?" she asked as she poked my abdomen viciously with her portable vibrator.

"Sounds very 'boyish' at the moment," she announced confidently as she monitored the baby's heart rate.

Exactly two weeks and two days following the amniocentesis, the results arrived in an official-looking brown envelope.

"Shall we open this together?" Mike asked, launching himself horizontally onto the bed, which created a catapult effect, sending my backside two feet off of the mattress and back down again.

Our baby had "no major chromosomal abnormalities," and we discovered that our baby was a girl. The midwife was wrong again.

I felt slightly triumphant in that I had reached nineteen weeks without any significant problems and that these results were another token of proof that advanced age alone doesn't automatically write a woman off to have a healthy pregnancy with a normal outcome.

During the third trimester, when I triumphantly strode into my antenatal appointments, my midwife was as jovial as ever.

"Oh dear. Rather a lot of glucose in your water. Better make a day-ward appointment for you to have a glucose tolerance test. Gestational diabetes can be more common in older mothers, you know," she chortled, forever reminding me that I was an antique. In fact, I didn't have diabetes. Were there any age-related conditions left to throw at me before I delivered my daughter?

"She's still lying with her spine to your spine," said the midwife at my thirty-seven-week appointment, after vigorously pressing around my lower abdomen and then announcing that she had been squashing the baby's cheeks. She shook her head and chuckled to herself whilst muttering something about a prolonged, backache labor.

"Of course, it is your fourth child and there's the age factor to consider," she said in her don't-say-I-didn't-warn-you type of voice. "You realize that because everything's stretched and not as firm as it used to be, it's more common for the baby to be lying in an awkward position."

Contrary to my midwife's pessimistic outlook, Lauren Erica was born safely after an uncomplicated and natural delivery.

Let the Professionals Do the Job

The midwife who delivered the baby, thankfully not the same one whom I visited throughout my pregnancy, marveled at how thick the umbilical cord was and how well nourished Lauren must have been.

The day following the birth, Lauren and I came home, both in excellent health.

Life with a young child has been uncomplicated and extremely rewarding. Apart from my breasts, which still enter the room half an hour before the rest of my body (not least because I am still breastfeeding my now three-year-old daughter), all my other vital organs have resumed their original and rightful positions. My abdomen still resembles a lump of dough that rolls over the top of my jeans when I try to zip them up.

Of course, it has nothing to do with my age!

Confessions of an Earth Mother Dropout

By Christy Lui

I started having Earth Mother fantasies when I first got pregnant. You know the kind — where you dream of doing it all naturally. Natural childbirth, organic foods, yoga, cloth diapers, home births, midwives and raspberry-leaf tea. I devoured a whole universe of books, pamphlets, magazines and Web sites devoted to convincing women that the process of delivering a child is something under their control.

Now I don't want to scare the stretchy pants off any new mom-to-be, but YOU HAVE NO CONTROL WHATSOEVER OVER THIS EXPERIENCE.

I know I'm going to hear it from the Lamaze instructors, the Bradley devotees and the natural childbirth Nazis, but I'm convinced it's all a big conspiracy to make women feel inadequate.

Oh sure, they say they're empowering you. They say you can choose how to deliver your baby. And C-sections are often unnecessary. They fill their books and magazines with quotes like "I delivered my ten-pound daughter underwater in thirty minutes by using a Vulcan Mind Meld with my midwife! It was pain-free!"

So, I went into my first son's birth convinced that preparation and determination were all it would take. Things started out just fine. I whooshed. I wheeshed. I centered my chakras. I connected to the Goddess.

After about six hours working an eight-pound baby down the birth canal (medication-free, to this point), the midwife arrived, did a quickie exam, pronounced me ten centimeters dilated and blanched.

Barely keeping the panic out of her voice, she yelled, "CALL THE DOCTOR NOW."

Apparently the baby's umbilical cord had slipped over the crown of his head, and any pushing was, well, life-threatening. They stole my glasses, and my gentle, life-affirming midwife took this opportunity to shove my eight-pound baby right back where he came from.

Let the Professionals Do the Job

I must have blacked out from pain, because my next memory is of being raced to the operating room, midwife elbow-deep, yelling, "FOR GOD'S SAKE, DON'T PUSH!"

Then, blissfully, they knocked me out, and I slept through the whole primal miracle of birth connection to the great circle of life thing.

You'd think I'd have learned from this experience that pain medication early-and-often was the way to go, but no, when my second son was due to arrive, I got sucked into the VBAC (vaginal birth after caesarean) propaganda. Sure, maybe my first birth wasn't ideal. But now I could redeem myself! The first complication was a fluke, definitely not something that would happen again. This time I'd reclaim the Earth Mother.

The VBAC instructor gave us lots of happy stories about how so many women were successful. Think on that. So if you don't have a successful VBAC, you are a failure?

My doctor smiled and said I had a seventy percent chance of a vaginal birth. Here's the big lie. That's in theory. In reality, the success rate of VBAC's is about twenty percent. I'm pretty sure the insurance companies see that as a pretty good margin. I'm all for avoiding surgery, but a thirty-minute wide-awake operation beats hell out of ten hours of labor (yes, oh yes, sans epidural, once again), three-and-a-half hours of pushing — followed by another C-section. At least I was awake for this one, but after nearly fourteen hours, I really didn't care.

And then, the aftermath. I didn't pay much attention during the C-section part of the childbirth classes. After all, Earth Mothers do not have C-sections. But I'm pretty sure they didn't cover these salient points: First, they won't feed you. I spent a great deal of time in labor promising myself a bacon cheese-burger, fries and a chocolate frozen-custard shake as soon as I squeezed the critter out.

I got Jello.

For two days.

You don't get to eat until you start making bowel sounds. Delicately phrased by the nurses as "passing gas." Nurses love to discuss gas passing at every opportunity, especially when the pastor of your church and your boss are visiting.

Second, the scar is positively frightening. Not only does your belly have the texture of a week-old latex balloon, but you also get the added bonus of a twelve-inch-long oozing welt punctuated every half inch by stainless-steel staples.

Then the drugs do weird things to your brain. I have no recollection of calling anyone after my second son's birth. My brother didn't know he was an uncle again for two days. I just forgot. I also made the mistake of not having a name picked out. When we got to the B's in the baby book, I was too tired and bored to continue.

To this day, I think my Benjamin should have been Charlie, but I was too whacked to put in the effort.

And recovering from a C-section is just not conducive to the Earth Mother ideal. I planned to spend my maternity leave energetically taking walks, cooking great meals (while, of course, losing the forty pounds I'd gained), creating a spectacular family scrapbook, painting the nursery with nontoxic paint and planting herbs in my garden. Instead, my weeks at home were spent reading murder mysteries and watching Oprah.

I then went back to work, abandoning nursing to the evils of formula (proper Earth Mothers nurse as long as they possibly can) and disposable diapers. (Earth Mothers launder their own cotton diapers in recycled water and hang them in the sun to dry.)

I still clung desperately to a few, last, lonely ideals — I made homemade baby food, freezing it into little cubes. I fed him tofu and avocados. When we moved to Wisconsin and I stayed home full time, I made my son homemade chicken nuggets and whole-wheat teething biscuits. Which he hated.

Now, having to deal on a day-to-day basis with two small children, I've tossed the old Earth Mother fantasy onto the compost heap. I am truly thankful for modern medicine and all the delightful painkillers that are available for childbirth. Instead of trying to live up to my fantasies, I've learned to rely on rationalization and excuses.

Maybe someday I'll reclaim the Earth Mother.

I hope I recognize her when the time comes.

"I Don't Know Nothin' 'Bout Birthin' Babies"

By Naida Lynn Wyckoff

Beautiful, slight of build and very Texan, Gloria had moved two years before to Eureka, California. Without pausing, she made a beeline straight into my heart and into the hippie community.

A month after her arrival, her son Bodie was born with the local free-clinic doctor in attendance, along with a room full of new acquaintances, eager to see a home birth. The delivery occurred on a mattress placed on an unhinged door laid on the backs of sawhorses. This gave the experience all the dignity of a livestock exhibit at the local county fair. What rescued it from the ridiculous was the main attraction, Bodie.

Losing contact with mother and babe for months, I was delighted with Gloria's reappearance and her move into the apartment across from me. In our building, a big, old house divided into units, we shared the top floor, front doors facing each other with nothing between us but a common bathroom and hallway.

As our friendship renewed, there was only one small wrinkle. Now, expecting her second child, Gloria wanted me to deliver this baby.

While I had birthed a few kittens in my days and had alarmed the hospital staff at the rapid delivery of my own child, I hardly felt qualified to deliver hers. Determined, she gave me a midwife training manual from England.

Reading it, "Earth Mother" that I was, I began to believe I could honor her request. That conviction disappeared when I got to the last chapter on complications. I gave the book back, suggesting a qualified midwife, Bill Fisher.

Bill agreed to accept Gloria, if she passed his intake test.

Standing on one leg, holding a strand of hair out from the side of her head, she succeeded. I had to agree with Bill on her general health. I figured any eight-month pregnant woman, who could balance on one foot while holding a piece of hair in the opposite hand was doing well.

That settled, I was off the hook.

I was to play a bit part in the supportive cast as coach.

Two weeks later, I awoke with Gloria standing at the foot of my bed asking, "Like some tea?" Sitting bolt upright, foggy with sleep, I stared at her then sank back on my pillow.

"Tea? Oh, I was hoping you were in labor."

Exasperated, Gloria said, "Naida, it is two o'clock in the morning! You don't really think I came for tea, do you?"

This was not a good start for a coach but I rallied quickly. Throwing off the covers, my feet were on the floor in one swift movement. We were back in her apartment in a hot second.

Gaining confidence, I settled into a chair. My smile was short lived. With contractions three minutes apart, Gloria was walking back and forth, hanging on her kitchen counter and huffing like a train at full speed. Alarmed and wanting to avoid a train wreck, I called Bill.

"Bill," I said, "she's on a roll."

I was relieved to hear his nonchalant "I'll be right over."

Still, Bill needed a little time to get things together and drive to our place. Not "right over" enough for me, but it would have to do. He'll be here soon, I reasoned. I busied myself laying out the necessary supplies and, in true frontier fashion, boiling water.

Checking on Gloria, I was not reassured by what I saw. White knuckling herself around the room, she was making noises I didn't much care for. Suggesting she lie down, I called Bill again.

"Yes?" The sound of Bill's voice on the other end of the phone was not a comfort.

"Bill," I said, "Gloria's in transition." Fortunately, I retain what I read and have very good instincts.

"Okay," he answered, "I am on my way."

Now Gloria was lying on the mattress on her side with feet and hands pressed against the wall, looking every bit like a spider on a web. I placed my hands gently on her back. Menacing guttural sounds emanated from her. Fearing for my life, my ill-placed hands were quickly removed.

"Definitely close," I thought.

With Bill just leaving, my concerns heightened. "Should I call an ambulance?" I asked.

Rolling on her back, Gloria said, "Too late, you catch and I'll push."

It didn't take a second glance to agree with her. Our supplies were in the other room, so we did without. Working as a team, the baby crowned, rotated and was born into my hands. "It's a girl!" I announced. Dark hair and fair skinned, Clover was a beauty.

Retrieving a large bowl from the kitchen, I said, "We'll use this for the placenta."

That done and not having sterile scissors to cut the cord, I placed the bowl with the placenta next to the infant. Gently, I swaddled her in a quilt.

Smiling, I mused that Gloria had gotten her way after all.

The sun was just coming up when Bill arrived. Approvingly, he looked mom and baby over, tied off the cord and handed me the scissors to do the honors. Then he said, "Good job. I'd like to train you."

Laughing, I said, "No thanks. Once was enough."

Two weeks later, I took Gloria to the county courthouse to record the birth. When she returned to the car, she handed me the birth certificate. Name, Sex of Baby, Name of Parents and Date of Birth, all typed in their boxes. In the space titled, Person Attending the Birth, was my name. "Pretty neat," I thought.

Next to it read, "Attending Person's Title: PDQ."

Puzzled, I turned to Gloria and asked, "I have a title? What does 'PDQ' stand for?"

Without hesitating, Gloria responded, "Pretty Damn Quick."

What They Don't Tell You about the Time to Push

By Jackie Buxton

I don't know about you, but I have a bit of a problem with pooing in public. In fact, I can safely say nobody has ever caught me with my pants down. I have a cozy life history of finding the right moment, politely excusing myself from my company, locking the door and doing the business.

So it won't surprise you to know that of all the things that filled me with horror about childbirth, having a poo in labor was king.

After graphic descriptions in antenatal classes of the body's sudden need to go, gentle soothing about the fact that most people do it (is that supposed to help?) and the fact that it's quickly swept away in a paper towel (and what, pray, do they do with the smell?), my birth plan went something like this: Give me pain. Give me sickness. Give me the sweat, the screaming, the feeling that if you push any harder your bones will break.

Just please, God, don't let me poo on the bed.

So you can imagine my distress when, six months into my excited first pregnancy, I'm told about my iron deficiency. A bit of iron going amiss wouldn't normally bother me. I was sick every day and still felt blooming. But I knew all about iron tablets — my blood would have more oxygen, I'd have renewed energy, I'd feel great!

But I'd be constipated.

And as far as I was concerned, my best chance of a pooless labor had been to get all of the damn stuff out of me before the show started. Constipation would throw a great, big, smelly spanner into the works.

"I don't need iron tablets," I valiantly explained to the doctor. "I'll be better. I'll drink less tea and coffee. I'll drink fresh orange juice with my meals. I'll add spinach to my cereal (hey! I'm pregnant, we can do any food combination)."

Let the Professionals Do the Job

And off I went with diet sheet in hand. It didn't work. A month later, my tail between my legs and a box of Pregaday™ in my hand, I left the doctor's to inflict my self-induced nightmare.

I took the tablets. Sales of oranges, apples, plums, raisins, grapes and bran hit fever pitch in our town. Two days before I went into labor, I hadn't been to the toilet for two days.

For any of you out there who haven't been through labor, I'd like to be the one to tell you that, actually, it isn't all bad. No, really. For the first few hours, my husband and I were pretty much left to our own devices. It was busy. It was December and we were nicknamed Mary and Joseph because, frankly, there was no room left at the inn. We were taken to the freezing back-up surgery, which hadn't been opened, let alone used, for months, and some borrowed gas and air was rigged up for me.

And then I think we were forgotten.

But we didn't care. We liked being alone. We rocked together on a birthing ball. We got excited. We felt very together. My husband had watched the midwives check the baby's heart rate. So he expertly rubbed gel on my stomach from time to time, deftly placed said instrument over the baby's heart and told me the baby was fine, with a heart rate between 120 and 160. My husband, by the way, is a call center manager. I have to say, his medical prowess impressed me, even in labor.

So it was great. We could manage. Our firstborn was on its way out. Would it be Elizabeth? Or would it be Tom?

When I say it was great, I must just qualify — except for one thing.

"John! I need a poo!"

"That's fantastic," adoring husband replied, "that means you're ready to push! That's what the antenatal woman said it would feel like!"

"No, it doesn't. It means I need a poo."

"What if the baby comes out as well? There's no one here!"

Oh, if it were only that easy.

"I don't care," I selfishly replied. "If I don't have a poo, I will explode!"

My contractions were a minute apart. The idea of leaving the back-up surgery, locating a toilet and walking to it without my beloved gas and air was marginally more horrific than the idea of having a poo right there and then in the middle of the back-up surgery floor. But my waters hadn't yet broken. There was still a fair way along the pain barometer to go. So I still had a modicum of self-awareness.

"Get me something to do it in!" I ordered.

Disused back-up surgeries, we found, don't have many empty vessels. In fact, they don't have much of anything apart from a bed and expensive-looking apparatus.

But they do have sick bowls.

We knew about sick bowls. For reasons we never quite understood, they were made from thick, gray cardboard and about the size of a small-headed person's hat. On each of my previous sickness bouts, I'd used an average of three.

"Sit on this!" My able birthing partner demanded.

I felt the need to explain to him that the baby, its home, my increased-width bottom and me probably wouldn't be able to perch too successfully. I was sentient enough to know my impromptu toilet would tip up, depositing my poo all over the pristine white tiles.

So, in between stoic hand-holding and rocking through contractions, my husband made me a toilet. He was always good at do-it-yourself, and this was his finest achievement to date. Directly in the center of a chair, he placed the said sick bowl. Around the bowl to support it, he placed a further selection of sick bowls filled with boxes of surgical gloves to weigh them down. Perfect.

"I'm going to have to go NOW!" I bellowed mid-way through the next contraction.

"As soon as this one's over," he soothed.

He raised me up to my throne and placed me on. With the weighted down sick bowls and his hands firmly placed on either side of the makeshift toilet, I was just about balanced.

"Ooooh!" I moaned as the poo made its way out. Next to our baby entering the world, this was the sweetest moment.

Let the Professionals Do the Job

Well, it should have been.

With my loudest groan of delight, the door swung open. Opposite me in my moment of pleasure was the new midwife. She hadn't met me before. She'd just changed shifts. Except she was newly qualified, so next to her was her support, an older midwife. Because the hospital staff were concerned I'd been somewhat abandoned, for good measure, next to her was a him.

The on-duty doctor had come to have a look.

So the room filled with the stench. Four people lifted me from my throne. My toilet was whisked away, somebody, I don't know who, was kind enough to wipe my bottom.

"I wonder," said the more experienced midwife, "you might be ready to push."

Part Six

I'm Afraid
It Pains Me to Say This

... when the urge to push is countered only by the feeling that it may smart when the beach ball you desperately want on the outside has to pass through the equivalent of a drinking straw to get there.

False Labor Pains a Real Pain

By Barbara David

"Well, no, nothing yet," the doctor said snapping off his latex gloves and handing me a wad of tissues.

"Nothing?" I asked, lunging my shoulders forward. I hoped the momentum might help my very pregnant body gain a sitting position.

"Maybe you're dilated a fingertip."

"A fingertip?" I knew he was trying to be kind. I braced on my elbows. "I really think I've been having contractions all day."

"Uh, well. False labor." He tossed the gloves in the trash and made a note on my chart, perhaps writing "fingertip" and drawing a smiley face beside it.

The nurse finally pulled me forward so I could sit.

"Is this your first baby?" she asked.

Did she mean only a first-timer could be fooled by false labor?

"No, my third," I said.

"Oh, well, then you know what to expect."

People kept saying that. I always pretended to agree, but really besides generalized pain and constant fatigue, I wasn't sure what to expect. I wondered how many people had done something twice and were considered experts.

I left the doctor's office and contractions, or what I thought were contractions, continued. I took care of my kids, did my best with the house and kept my husband and parents posted on the pain. One evening, after a day of constant, close contractions, I called the doctor. I told him my name and described my pain.

"When's your due date?" he asked. I could tell he was unimpressed.

"In two weeks," I moaned, trying to put a sense of urgency in my voice.

"We still have at least fourteen more days."

He wasn't leaving his living room.

"Drink eight glasses of water and walk around the house. When you go to sleep, lie on your left side."

"If I drink eight glasses of water I won't go sleep."

"You can call in the morning if you want."

So I spent the night in the bathroom, not the delivery room.

Still, my bed and bathroom beat the two trips to the hospital with the humiliating homecomings. All day, gut-wrenching, back-throbbing pain. After hours of semi-silent suffering, I called the doctor.

"Okay," he sighed. "Check in at triage and they'll monitor your progress. I'll be in contact."

My heart soared. "Yes! We're going to have the baby!" I hugged the kids. Called Mom and Dad to babysit. I got my stuff together and happily hopped in the van.

And the contractions stopped.

I tried to pretend something was happening. I felt a little movement. A kick. A squirm. Something that might be a contraction.

But I knew.

Through the streets, the parking garage, the maze of hospital hallways, I prayed for pain.

We registered with the receptionist and eventually she asked, "Are you having contractions now?"

I hesitated. Come on, contraction. Come on. I took a deep breath. "Well, no. Not right now."

"Were you before?"

"Yes, all day."

"Uh, huh," she noted with smiling condescension. Here it comes, I thought. "Is this your first baby?"

"No, third."

"Oh, well. Then you know what to expect. The nurse will take you to the monitoring room."

The nurse took us to a small room before I could explain.

I'm Afraid It Pains Me to Say This

I wanted to go back and just say that my water broke with my first, and my second was a week late and I just went into labor. The contractions were contractions and they just came and . . .

My husband's voice interrupted my mental monologue. "So, you're not having contractions?"

I realize now it was an innocent question asked by a curious, loving father who had rearranged his work schedule for his wife who said she was having a baby. However, at the time it seemed like an evil, mean-spirited accusation. He waited for my answer.

Of course, I burst into tears.

The nurse arrived and I summoned my high school acting abilities to feign happiness. Apparently I wasted my junior and senior years in the Masque and Gavel Drama Society. I didn't look happy.

"Been crying?" she asked, handing me some tissues. "Late-term hormones," she said, sparing me from telling the truth and spilling more tears.

She fastened a belt and monitor around my mammoth middle and propped me on my left side. "Now we'll see what's going on." She flipped a switch and left the room.

The machine started blipping and beating. My husband and I took comfort in watching our son's measured heartbeat. A graph also showed the level and frequency of contractions: none. A straight line continued across the screen and mocked me by printing itself on a long sheet of paper. I imagined a group of doctors and nurses gathered in the break room with my record of straight-line contractions. They'd look at my graph and laugh. Gasping for breath between great guffaws, one of them would silence the group for a moment and say, "And this is her third!" The hospital would rock with hilarity.

Uncomfortable with the image and my position, I moved just a bit. Moments later, the straight line started inching upward. A hill, then a mountain. Another and another! My husband noticed too, "Hey that's a big one!"

The nurse rushed in. I thought, "This is it."

"You moved," she said, and readjusted the belt, reducing the mountains to less than mole hills.

About an hour later, we went home.

And about a week later, we did it all again.

Finally, I vowed to avoid the hospital until I saw the baby's head. Fortunately, the doctor felt sorry for me before that moment, and decided to induce. Modern medicine made the contractions real, and at last the ordeal gave birth to our wonderful baby boy. He was welcomed by his big brother and sister, and later joined by two more brothers. These two embryonic pranksters also enjoyed teasing me with contractions that just didn't deliver, but their third trimester tricks didn't matter — once I delivered them.

Dead Serious

By Penny Aicardi

All right. It may seem silly, especially in this day and age, but I've always been afraid of death when it comes to childbirth. I had a C-section with my first, and had planned a repeat section for my second. Although I knew everything that was going to happen the worst always seemed to run through my mind: What if I have a blood clot? What if the doctor leaves some foot-long pry bar inside my stomach? What if I get a deadly bacterial infection from that foot-long pry bar? Don't laugh, I saw that very scenario on television once.

Despite my fear, I was about to have my second child, when my doctor handed me a health-care proxy. It seemed simple enough: pick someone to make my health-care decisions for me should the occasion arise that I couldn't. My husband was the obvious choice. But when I went home and started to discuss the issue I discovered his views about what I wanted doctors to do in an emergency situation were about as misconstrued as mine were about why he should sit inside on a sunny 75-degree day watching a NASCAR race on television instead of taping it for later.

"I'd tell them not to revive you," he told me calmly, but dead (no pun intended) serious. Mistakenly, I had opted to discuss this over dinner at my parents' house. Everyone was there, and no one even looked up when he said it.

Now, the pregnancy hormones probably made me overreact a bit, but I couldn't help but scream out, "What?"

I looked at him with dismay and wondered what the hell he was thinking.

"You are kidding me, right?" I asked.

"No. Why would you want to be a vegetable all your life?"

"Maybe your brain is on those carrots you're eating," I said sarcastically. "But right now, mine is on staying alive! I'm not going to be a vegetable and I'm certainly not going to be dead!"

By now, the conversation had gathered some attention. My mother and sister found it hilarious, while my brother-in-law adamantly agreed with my husband. Everyone had an opinion. But wait! It wasn't *my* opinion. This is just great! Everyone wants to put me in my grave! Imagine the horror if I hadn't discussed this with my family prior to my C-section. I guess I wouldn't be able to since I would be dead!

Okay, that was it. My mind was made up. I announced that I was not going to name my husband as my health-care proxy — not now, not ever. My mother was pretty silent, my sister continued to laugh and my father just ignored the entire scenario.

My husband told me I was being ridiculous.

After that night, we didn't discuss the health-care proxy again. I really wasn't sure what I was going to do. I knew another discussion was needed to resolve the issue. Unfortunately, my son Jason didn't give us that chance. I went into labor two days later, and like every woman dreams, it was pretty fast.

I awoke at 6 a.m. to the alarm clock, and before I could even get out of bed, my water broke. I called my mother and told her we were bringing my daughter to her house. After dropping her off, I went straight to the hospital. Less than an hour later the contractions had really kicked in. The doctor informed me that I would be in surgery within the hour. I wasn't even thinking of the health-care proxy.

"Breathe, breathe, breathe," my husband, trying to be helpful, was ranting.

"Do you have an allergy to latex?" the nurse asked me in the middle of a contraction. "Let's answer the questions when the contraction passes. And, Mr. Aicardi, does your wife have the health-care proxy form with her?"

Suddenly, no contraction seemed that unbearable.

"No!" I screamed. "Whatever you do, save my life! I don't care what it takes!"

The room went silent and everyone just glared at me.

"What? Did everyone forget I'm having a baby here!" I yelled.

Everyone went on with their routines and the surgery went

I'm Afraid It Pains Me to Say This

well. As they were rolling me out of the operating room, I breathed a sigh of relief. "Thank God. I'm alive."

"And all without a health-care proxy," the nurse said before breaking out into laughter.

Call a Pain a Pain

By Dorothea Helms

Dr. Lamaze should have been a woman. A pregnant woman. A bloated, ankle-sore, blotchy, constipated, skin-stretched-to-its-limit, hormones-out-of-whack, tired of Shamu the Killer Whale jokes, nine-months pregnant woman.

And, he should have gone into labor. Hard labor. Back-breaking transition labor, when the urge to push is countered only by the feeling that it may smart when the beach ball you desperately want on the outside has to pass through the equivalent of a drinking straw to get there.

Everyone responsible for La Leche League advertising should try breastfeeding for the first time, and experience what it's like to have a sucking 12-amp vacuum-cleaner hose hooked up to his or her nipples.

Paranoia is not my usual state. My eldest child is twenty-seven years old, so I'll grant you that the memories of my first child-birthing experience are somewhat sketchy. I do remember the progression of the labor, and all the visual, auditory and kinesthetic images came flooding back recently when I read an article by a young woman who gave birth and started breast-feeding, and who was shocked at how much pain the entire process entailed.

Whoops! I said the "P" word.

As a graduate of the Lamaze Method of Childbirth, I was told to refer to the labor things as contractions or pressure. I believed that when I took the classes with my husband, acting as coach, in 1975. Imagine my surprise when the first few initial contractions progressed into down-and-dirty labor and caused me — yes, PAIN!

I was afraid to say it hurt, because we were doing so well with the shallow breathing, coaching and ice chips on the lips. I'd always been an "A student." I couldn't imagine failing the Lamaze method by screaming at the smiling hospital personnel and calling my husband a mewling, beef-witted horned beast, so

I'm Afraid It Pains Me to Say This

I grinned, breathed and bore it — literally — and we had a son.

Seven years later, I found myself on the delivery table once again, this time having our daughter with a different doctor in attendance. As I lay there, coping with contractions and dining on slivers of ice, it happened: my most cherished childbirth moment. My doctor asked me how strong the pains were. My shocked husband asked why the doctor called the contractions "pains."

The MD looked at me and asked, "Dorothea, how do you feel?"

In the middle of a contraction, I, a now more liberated woman, snarled, "It hurts like hell."

"That's why I call them pains," he said.

Now, why couldn't Dr. Fernand Lamaze, the fanatic who introduced his famous birthing method to France in 1951 after a trip to Russia, be as straightforward? I mean, who ever heard of a Russian admitting to pain?

Imagine my further mothering surprise when I started breastfeeding my first child and it hurt! I read the La Leche League book and went to a couple meetings to prepare myself for the glorious experience. I remember a plethora of words thrown at me: bonding, colostrum and even the touching fact that La Leche League's name is derived from the Spanish words for "the milk." But no one told me that the first few times the baby latched on, I'd be ready to take off through the roof from the pain.

Lamaze — La Leche — the coincidence is just too weird. I've decided to coin my own word for my preferred method of giving birth: La Truth. The Lamaze method of childbirth works, and it's great. Within a few minutes of pushing out that bundle of joy, you feel euphoric, and there are no sluggish, drug after effects to deal with if you complete natural childbirth. But contractions hurt. According to the La Truth method, there's no reason to not know this when going into labor and delivery.

What La Leche League teaches about breastfeeding is vital, but La Truth wants you to know that nursing will bring an initial reaction of something quite the opposite of pleasure. The pain may be worthwhile. For most women it's temporary, and it's a small price to pay for the convenience, cost savings and health benefits of feeding your child the natural way.

And to tell you La Truth, natural childbirth taught me a lot about life. I remember another second-time-around delivery-room scene with my doctor. In the midst of a major contraction I said, "Come on, baby, you're doing great!"

My surprised physician said, "You're approaching all of this with an amazingly positive attitude."

"I figure every pain is a step closer to birth," was my reply.

I've often thought of that sentiment when I've faced hard-ships. Granted there's a lot of pain out there that leads to death, not life. Some is preventable, like war. Some is unpredictable and insidious, like cancer. And some we bring on ourselves. La Truth means figure out which it is. Eliminate it, if you can, and find something positive in it if you can't.

And remember that natural childbirth and breastfeeding aren't the last times you'll feel pain as a mother.

But someday soon enough, that beach ball will place a hand on your shoulder and say, "Here Mom, let me get that for you." And then the memory of labor and breastfeeding pain will fade just a little bit more.

And that's La Truth!

Part Seven

Now Arriving in Gate A

I assumed I'd have a chance to rest between contractions. Maybe have a glass of ice tea. Marvel with my husband about the magical journey we were about to embark on.

Wheelman

By Nadine Meeker

My husband was stationed at Fort Knox as a US Army M1 tanker and we lived off base. My mother had come down two weeks prior to my due date to visit and help out after the baby was born because we knew it would be a C-section.

The baby was due on June 4th. My husband called the afternoon before around 4:30 p.m. and said he would be coming home late that evening. We hung up and not more than five minutes later, I went into labor — hard labor. At first I brushed it off as false labor that I had experienced two weeks earlier.

But this time was much different.

When the contractions began coming about three minutes apart in only fifteen minutes, my mother was convinced this was for real. After having read tons of baby books, I knew labor took anywhere from eight to ten hours minimum for a first-time mom like me, so I had lots of time. Right? Right!

But I also knew contractions built slowly over time. They don't just sucker punch you and leave you in pain for long stretches that soon. They were supposed to build slowly so you experience the joys of natural childbirth with a slight breather in between each one. I wasn't getting any breathers. I knew from the pain I was having and how quickly it was coming that something was definitely odd.

At my mother's insistence, I called my husband back at quarter to five and told him I was heading up to the hospital.

He offered to come home and get me, but again, my mom suggested he meet us there, since he was already on base. In truth, she didn't think we had enough time, but she didn't tell him for fear he'd race over and get himself hurt. At this point, my contractions were about two minutes apart.

So with her daughter in tow and a grandbaby on the way, my mother helped me to her nice, new car and we drove to the post at a steady pace. When you come in and out of the base, you have a checkpoint to pass. Upon seeing my overgrown, clutched stomach they let us right inside and gave me a "good luck little lady." By this time, it was 5 p.m. and the pain was intense. Contractions were a minute apart, if that.

We came up to the traffic light near the hospital, but no one moved, even after the traffic light changed. My mom looked around to find out what the hold up was. My first thought (aside from, I'm-never-going-to-let-my-husband-touch-me-again) was that maybe there was an accident. But I remembered, some-where in my pain-riddled mind, that the MPs stop traffic so everyone can salute the flag at 5 p.m.

It's not an option.

You have to stop, and if you don't it's not pretty, so my mother asked me, "What do I do?" just as another contraction hit me.

"Get to the hospital," I told her.

With tires screeching, she pulled around the stopped traffic and flew past the MP. I looked behind to see him dash to his car. Sure enough, he gave chase, sirens blaring. My mom raced through the driveway toward the front entrance and we passed my husband who was sitting in his truck, waiting for our arrival.

I'll never forget the look on his face as he watched his out-law wife and mother-in-law trying to outrun the MP. His eyes practically left their sockets and he bruised his jaw on the truck door as he watched us speed by.

As my mom came to a stop, we opened the doors and jumped out. Well, she jumped out. I kind of heaved myself to the sidewalk. My husband was running faster than I've ever seen him move before or since. The MP was now out of his car asking my mom if there was an emergency.

Hello?! Pregnant woman who can barely stand over here.

My husband spoke and that's when the MP noticed me. Before my husband could finish, the MP smiled and nodded. And again, I got a "Good luck little lady."

At that point I didn't need luck. I needed a doctor.

When we finally made it to the child-birthing area, I was dilated to five centimeters and within the next half hour I was at

Now Arriving in Gate A

a full ten and ready to have this kid one way or another. Instead of the wave of contractions all the books had told me about, the last half hour was just one constant pain.

At 6:28 p.m. — after two hours of labor and three-and-a-half hours before her due date — our daughter, Eryn, was born. It was the first and last moment she was ever on time in her life.

Who knows? Maybe someday, if my daughter decides to have children, I might become the wheelman.

Express Delivery

By Irene A. Pileggi

Pregnant with my third child, my doctors always told me to make sure I was in close proximity to the hospital, as I could go into labor at any time and have a quick birth.

Little did they know …

It was about 6:00 a.m. on a Saturday morning. I started feeling contractions, minutes apart, but painful. I lived just five miles from the hospital and had a reliable family member who would come at any given second to stay with the children, so I didn't really panic yet.

At about 7:30 a.m., the contractions seemed nonstop. We called for my sister-in-law to come over, and she set out on the thirty-minute drive. After ten minutes of waiting, we knew we were going to have to pack up the children in the car and go to the hospital or give birth in the house.

When we got to the hospital, my husband ran in to get a wheelchair for me. He wasn't quick enough. I started beeping the horn and screaming at top of my lungs for help.

When hubby FINALLY came back out, a candy striper put me in a wheelchair and we were off to the labor room, while he parked the car and brought the kids into the waiting area.

Little did we both know …

Before we reached the elevators, my water broke. As soon as we were out of the elevators, I felt the baby pushing.

Three nurses rushed me to the labor room. While they prepared the bed for me, the baby's head popped out … followed by the body.

My baby girl was born in my pink lace panties!

Well, Officer, It's Like This …

By Virginia Heffernan

The immediate neighbors had been warned. "If you hear screams coming from our house within the next couple of weeks, don't worry, it's just me having a baby."

Since the midwives considered my pregnancy low-risk and the hospitals were close by, we'd decided on a home birth. We liked the idea of relaxing in our own bed with wine and cheese after the hard work was over, then slipping into a deep sleep with our baby between us.

It would be peaceful, tranquil and even fun.

Right.

The first pangs of labor hit during a blistering day in early July. Within a couple of hours, Graham was ready to make his debut, but we didn't appreciate the urgency of our situation. Roger made a routine call to our midwife to tell her I was progressing nicely. She asked him to point the mouthpiece in my direction so she could better judge the sound effects. To her experienced ear, I sounded like a woman in the final stages of labor.

"I'm on my way," she shouted into the phone.

By the time she arrived, I was digging my nails into Roger's back and cursing like an angry teenager. The screams radiated out the open windows and into the hot, still night.

Meanwhile, my brother-in-law David was holding the fort two floors down in our Victorian duplex, trying to block out the screams with a video. He was halfway through *Cliffhanger* when he heard a loud knock at the door. Standing on the porch was a trio of police officers dressed in riot gear. They said they were responding to calls that an assault was taking place in our home. He laughed and began to explain.

"I'm sorry, Sir. We have to see for ourselves," the lead officer interrupted, as he swept David aside and led the charge up the first flight of stairs to the second-floor landing.

"The cops are coming," David called up to the birth party congregated on the third floor.

One of the midwives, sporting a white dress smeared with blood, moved quickly to intercept. Having seen more than enough to confirm their suspicions, the police were ready to draw their guns when, thankfully, Graham entered the world and let out some healthy wails of his own. He saved the day. The cops backed down and left the scene of the crime.

Next time, I'll warn the distant neighbors too.

Not as Advertised

By Kira Vermond

They promised me I would be able to shave my legs between contractions. They promised!

Oh, all right. Maybe they never actually promised, but more than a few calm moms had told me I'd have enough time to shave before heading off to the hospital. I needed to believe it. My own personal hell included stubbly legs up in stirrups, for all the room to see.

So there I was, standing in the shower, trembling and moaning as one contraction after another wrung my uterus out like a dishrag. Clutching my pink razor like it alone would prevent me from being pulled down under the pain's tow, I swore to God I was going to have a word with those failed soothsayers.

Shave my legs? Ha! I'd shave their heads.

This wasn't turning out as I'd had it planned at all. I mean, really. How was I supposed to know labor pains would kick off at a leisurely twelve to fifteen minutes apart, only to gain momentum like the train roaring down the track?

I assumed I'd have a chance to rest between contractions. Maybe have a glass of ice tea. Marvel with my husband about the magical journey we were about to embark on.

How could I have been so thick?

Instead, there was Dave on the other side of the shower curtain with the pathetic little sheet of paper they'd given us in the prenatal class. We were supposed to use it to chart how far apart the contractions were. It had seemed so logical in class. Labor was something that could be quantified after all.

But, of course I was wrong, wrong, wrong.

"Are you sure you don't want to get out of the shower, honey?" Dave asked me tentatively as contraction after contraction threw me against the stall.

"I'm almost done the first one," I answered tersely, even

though I wasn't.

"This is crazy," Dave finally said. "No one is going to care if your legs are hairy. Dr. Brooks won't care. Your family won't care. I certainly won't care. Besides," he said, "we won't be looking at your legs."

That was cold, cold comfort.

But I eventually took his hand and stepped away from the water. And he was right. I felt a lot better, although I still applied a little lip gloss before leaving the room.

As each contraction rose and fell, Dave charted it all:

Time contraction starts: 3:12 a.m.

Duration: 30 seconds

Frequency: 12 minutes apart

Comments: Not strong. Lots of time before hospital.

And then:

Time contraction starts: 5:01 a.m.

Duration: 60 seconds

Frequency: 2 minutes apart

Comments: Big. BIG! (10 out of 10) What do we do now???

We eventually did the only thing we could think of. We called our friends Lisa and Jeff, both doctors, who quite sportingly offered to let us ring them if we had questions.

"Day or night," they said. "Don't worry. We're used to it."

So we called them. Dave, sitting on the bed, telling Jeff about my contractions like they were planning a trip to watch a game, and me pacing back and forth saying, "Tell him my water broke. Tell him I broke my water."

Finally he did. "Oh, and by the way, her water broke."

Jeff's voice suddenly exploded over the phone, reaching me like shrapnel from across the room. "Go! Go now! Get to the hospital now!"

So we went.

And everything was fast and intense and fine. I didn't even remember the hairy leg until the next day standing in the hospital's shower stall. I looked down beyond my accordion tummy

Now Arriving in Gate A

and saw a set of gams as mismatched as a pair of wayward socks.

But you know, it looked pretty swell.

I'd earned my right to be imperfect.

My Dad's Delivery

By Melinda Jones

My dad is the ultimate old-fashioned conservative. Growing up I never, ever heard him talk about sex or childbirth, or anything along those lines. If we were watching a movie that had a risqué scene, I would feel uncomfortable.

So when my sister and I began having children and bringing the babies over for visits, my dad had to face the fact that, yes, his daughters were, in fact, having sex.

It was just too much information for one poor man with two daughters, but he was a very good sport. He was calm and able to maintain his composure when we would nurse the babies in the living room. At first we did take them into the other room to give Dad time to adjust but that got to be too big of a hassle. Little did he know that his biggest challenge in his whole my-daughters-are-having-sex-and-procreating dilemma lay ahead.

When I was getting ready to have my second child, my husband, who is in the Navy, was not going to be able to be there for the birth. My parents got the call and came up to stay with me until the big day. A couple of days came and went and then one morning I woke up with slight contractions. They got stronger as the day went on and by late evening I was packing my bag.

My parents were still talking about who was going to take me to the hospital and who was going to stay with my daughter when I finally put my foot down, got the keys and said, "Make up your minds, I need to go and I really don't think that you want me to drive myself."

By default, my dad was appointed my official hospital escort and cheerleader. Although Mom and Dad had five kids, Dad had never been allowed to be with her at any of the births. Dad was in the room when my niece was born, but so were about fifty other people, and my sister said that he was fidgeting in the back corner for most of the time.

"Are you sure you really need me there?" my dad asked.

"Dad ...!" I said as incredulously as possible.

"Okay. Okay. Just checking. Let's go."

We got to the hospital a little after 10:00 p.m. and they put me in the admitting room. Dad waited outside while the doctor checked my progress. They decided to admit me and we were whisked away to the room.

My dad sat patiently with me, giving me my ice chips, wiping my forehead and making idle conversation. When the doctors came in to check my dilation, they were very discreet and tried to leave me some shred of modesty (as much as one can have when your legs are up to your ears and spread for all the world to see). Dad listened intently when the anesthesiologist came in and explained what he was going to do, and my father let me squeeze his hand till it was about to break when I was told to hold still.

When it came time to finally push, the nurse had me do a couple of practice pushes to see what would happen. I told her that the last time I did this, they had to run and find the doctor quickly and made me stop pushing.

The nurse kind of gave a little laugh as if to say, "Yeah, I am sure that's what happened."

Sure enough after two practice pushes, they told me to stop and ran to get the doctor.

When the doctor came in, the nurse was organizing everyone, and my dad, who had kept post up by my head, was called to the front lines.

She looked at him and said, "Okay, Grandpa, grab a leg, it's time to have a baby."

I swear that all of the color in my dad's face disappeared and his jaw hit the floor.

By this time, I honestly couldn't care less who was holding my leg as long as someone grabbed the darned thing so that I could get on with the show. He paused momentarily, stammering a bit, and the nurse urged him on.

My dad was such a trooper that morning. He grabbed that leg, looked me in the eyes, and his grandson was born ten minutes later.

I don't recall Dad's reaction when Andrew was born, but I do remember him declining to cut the umbilical cord (hey, one step at a time). Dad made the calls to the family, admired his grandson and waited by my side until things settled down. Then, he wearily said good-bye, promising to return with my mom and daughter later and threatening to send my husband a bill for the delivery when he got home.

I know it was never my dad's intention to actually be a part of the delivery. Even though I was more than a bit uncomfortable at the thought of my dad being in the delivery room — although probably not as much as he was — I am so happy and relieved that he was. The only thing that my dad has said about the experience is that it was "very intense." And now, Andrew's grandpa loves to tell him how he was the first to see him, even before his mommy.

My Perfect Plan for a Perfect Birth
By Tamara Talbot

Birthing class is a strange experience. You sit with a group of complete strangers discussing hemorrhoids and sex, when the only thing you truly have in common is that you will all, at some point, be giving birth.

The most important lesson I learned from attending these classes was the significance of creating a birth plan. Everyone who wants the perfect birth must have the perfect birth plan. After all, those who fail to plan, plan to fail.

I planned to have the perfect birth. The perfect birth didn't plan to come along for the ride.

I was sitting on the toilet — a popular place for me during my eighth month of pregnancy — looking down at my mildly damp, extremely large underwear, wondering, "Is that amniotic fluid, maybe a trickle, or did I just pee myself?"

At that point in my pregnancy, it could have just as easily been either one.

When pregnant, particularly for the first time, you fear that somehow you'll miss it — miss the labor — miss the contractions — miss the water breaking or trickling. I pulled up my underwear, hurried out of the bathroom and ran into my boss's office, a seasoned pro and recent mother of two children.

"Call the hospital and tell them you're on the way, Tamara. It's the safe thing to do — go."

With that, I called my husband, Todd, and we set off for the hospital. I was excited to be there and shuffled into the observation room for tests. I lay patiently, pain-free (unlike my co-pregnants in the other rooms), waiting in my hospital gown until a nurse finally appeared. She pulled out a test strip to see if there were any signs of amniotic fluid, I pulled back my hospital gown.

"No, definitely not, probably just urine," she said.

I must have looked disappointed. She reassured me that my time would come and that at thirty-six weeks the baby is not fully developed, so it was best she stay in the oven as long as possible. Just to further reassure me, the nurse decided to do an internal. Glove on and in she went — poking and prodding while I lay in obvious discomfort — out came the hand with a warm gush. I looked down, blood was everywhere and cramping began almost immediately.

The nurse accidentally began the premature effacing of my cervix and I was immediately racing at full speed down the road to an early labor. Panic quickly pulled in to join me in the race.

None of this was in my perfect birth plan for my perfect birthing experience. For the next two days, I fought labor with morphine and bed rest. The contractions subsided and I was sent home.

"No more work, take it easy, relax and put your feet up."

And that's exactly what I did … right up to my due date.

To celebrate the due date, and to take my mind off the fact that the baby STILL hadn't arrived, my husband took me out for a fantastic dinner.

I awoke the next day with what I thought was constipation. I told Todd that this could be it, but was still uncertain. One hour later, I was in the shower and the wave hit again, this time longer and definitely painful.

OK, this is it!

I called my mom, who said, "Take a walk, go grocery shopping, keep your mind off the pain, keep busy."

So — Todd and I did just that. We started with a neighborhood walk, contractions ten minutes apart and bearable. We decided to head to the grocery store — gotta stock up, need milk, bread and tea for the in-laws. We got to the mall and I couldn't even make it to the grocery store. The contractions were now five minutes apart and I was standing in a candy store facing the chocolates. People walked by assuming I was taking my time choosing the perfect chocolate, while in reality, I was writhing in pain and trying to maintain mall-friendly composure.

NO CHOCOLATES ON MY MIND!

Now Arriving in Gate A

We headed home — a very irritating ride. We went upstairs to pack trying to decide whether or not to go to the hospital when, WHOOSH — another warm flow, the bloody show, the whole bit.

Okay, I think that might just be a good indication that it was time to run to the hospital.

This time, as I was ushered into the observation room, I was nervous and scared. A nurse looked into my eyes, "Slow down, Tamara … slow down … breathe slowly … b r e a t h e … b r e a t h e."

Okay, the contraction ebbed.

The same nurse looked into my eyes again. "You're having a baby today, honey, whether you like it or not."

Suddenly the reality set in.

We're not in a restaurant. I can't change my order, tell them it's not what I hoped for, or simply leave. This is it. Ready or not, here she comes.

It was time to decide about the epidural. Hmmm … a pain-free birth versus an all-natural, all-feeling one?

"I'll take the epidural NOW please, thank you."

The next eight hours I chatted with friends and family while my husband watched the Stanley Cup play-offs on the huge television in my enormous birthing room.

The nurse came in. Once again, it was glove on and in she went.

I was dilated ten centimeters. Time to push. I was concerned about my relaxed state. Shouldn't I feel the need to push like so many others I had seen on the Learning Channel's *The Baby Story*? The nurse reassured me that with modern medicine there's no need, and that everything would be fine.

And the pushing began.

One hour later, after no progress, the doctor came in and was horrified at my epidural level.

"Feeling a little generous?" he ridiculed the nurse.

I was told to sit it out for a while until my feeling was … well … there.

Another hour passed and pushing recommenced. Pushing is a strange experience, surreal best describes it. Here I was, pushing a child out of me.

Natural they say. Not to me.

One hour of epidural-free pushing and burning and out popped Karley. I was so relieved she was out that I hardly noticed her odd coloring as they placed her on a table with doctors scurrying and pumping at her chest.

"Todd, you're in the way. Todd, move over, I can't see her!" I shouted.

What I didn't know was that Todd was trying to hide her lifeless body from me. After what seemed like an eternity, the crying every new mother yearns for suddenly filled the hospital room. Todd and I were in tears.

The commotion around us hadn't stopped. Nurses and doctors scurried about because apparently I was still bleeding. My placenta had not come out and I was feeling contractions again.

Boy ... was I pissed.

Hours and hours of labor, finally my baby girl is born and I'm having contractions! This is not fair!

My epidural had done its job... the first time, so they readministered it until I was frozen to the neck — gloves went on and in the doctor went, manually ripping my fresh stitches while up to his elbows.

With a yank, the doctor fell back and was holding something in the air.

"Oh my God. Look at this. The umbilical cord ripped completely free from the placenta!"

At this point, I was in no mood for show-and-tell.

I tried to show enthusiasm while every last bit was manually removed and the bleeding subsided. I was a few seconds from a blood transfusion.

Childbirth class didn't come close to preparing me for this experience. When I was visiting my ob-gyn months before, I started discussing my birth plan, when he cut me short.

Now Arriving in Gate A

"A little word of advice. Never plan your birth, because, guaranteed, it will not go as planned!"

I'm already planning not to plan next time.

Part Eight

It May Be Natural,
But It Ain't Easy

I looked at my little cherub
asleep in his bassinet.
He seems so beautiful when he sleeps
— when he's not gnawing
at my body.

In the Middle of the Night

By Christine Miles

"I will never feed that baby again."

To his credit, Derek didn't flinch. He looked at his firstborn, cradled in his arms, and then looked at me. The baby cried.

I cried.

That child had finished feeding only an hour before. He couldn't starve in an hour, could he? My breasts were so sore. Hugely swollen, nipples flattened to pancakes — ooze, ooze, ooze.

If it wasn't milk, it was blood. Owwww!

"Go and have a bath," Derek said. Relax for a bit. So I did. I will never say no to a bath. Blissful peace, only me in the bathroom.

For six minutes.

Derek was at the door saying, "The supermarket closes in half an hour. Shall I go and buy formula?"

The thought was so appealing, never again to expose my boobs in public, to be able to raise my arms above my head, and to be dry, with no sudden and unexpected floods of milk raining from my clothing.

But, formula is so expensive, and away I went, crying again.

Derek disappeared out of the room. He was soon back.

"Here. Read this."

He gave me my breastfeeding book. It seemed we had agreed to persist with breastfeeding.

An hour later, I heaved myself, wrinkled and cold, over the edge of the bath. Perhaps I could do this.

I looked at my little cherub asleep in his bassinet. He seems so beautiful when he sleeps — when he's not gnawing at my body.

I got to work. The sofa wouldn't work — it had to be a kitchen chair. Bolt upright. My legs had to be perpendicular to my body.

They weren't. (Since when did math come in to feeding the natural way?)

Two telephone books were stacked on the floor. I sat on the chair; my lap was perfect. I searched in the dark of the baby's room for a pillow to go on my lap. No way was that baby going to hang off my bosom.

The night-light was carefully positioned. A glass of water was on the table within easy reach. I consulted my breastfeeding book. I would also need a bib, a diaper, the wipes, the changing mat and my dressing gown.

I'd be all day putting things away tomorrow.

I went to bed. Please sleep through the night. Please, please.

He slept until one a.m. I cuddled and soothed as we prepared for THE FEED. Get this feed wrong and it wouldn't matter how much formula cost. The chair was hard and cold, the phonebooks were cold too (must get slippers), and why wouldn't the dressing gown stay closed over my legs? The pillow, the baby and the glow of the night-light on the other side of the room were the only warm bits. I snuggled against my baby, took a sip of water and consulted with the book one last time.

Okay. Now.

The tiniest bit of discomfort as the baby latched on.

Everything was perfect.

I thought smug thoughts. I didn't dare move — not even a smile.

Something moved. I could have sworn I saw something move out of the corner of my eye. I struggled to focus in the dimness, hoping and not hoping that I might see the movement again. Nothing. I looked at my baby, greedily guzzling, and out of the corner of my eye I saw it again. A movement. It was easier to focus this time.

Running across my living-room floor was a mouse.

"Derek," I whispered as loudly as I dared. "Derek." The baby guzzled happily onward, probably enjoying a decent feed more than I was.

Somehow, miraculously, Derek heard me. He rushed into the room. No doubt he expected to see a hysterical, babbling wife

It May Be Natural, But It Ain't Easy

weeping into her brassiere.

"It's a mouse," I said, still whispering.

In his sleep-muddled state, Derek didn't know what I was talking about.

Do I dare to talk aloud?

"Let the cat in."

The cat was useless. She chased the mouse around the room with no plan for catching it. The mouse ran behind the cabinet and straight up the wall.

My baby was feeding well. I would not tolerate a mouse in my house. I was empowered.

I detached my baby from my breast, exactly the way the book told me to. It didn't hurt. I wasn't stretched out like a big wad of bubble gum.

I gave my baby to my husband. I got the broom and pushed the stick behind the cabinet. The mouse wouldn't give in without a fight. I forced him out. I opened the front door and chased him out.

I chased the cat out too.

I took my baby from my husband and repositioned myself on the kitchen chair. I smiled at my baby and attached him to my other breast. The tiniest bit afraid, but confident, I smiled at Derek too. I'm sure he thought he was dreaming.

"Thanks for helping, honey. Go back to bed."

Breast Is Best

By Philippa Tite

Christopher was three months old, and with my maternity leave up, I had returned to work three days before. An exceptionally strong woman, I had been confident that I would handle the separation from my son with equanimity and calm.

But then, I've been wrong before.

After being back at work for three days, I felt I was slowly improving. On day one, I had sobbed the whole way from the day care to the office, had called them seventeen times by 11:30 a.m., and was sent home at 2 p.m. for being a wreck, and in the words of my boss, "completely useless to me".

Day two, I was better. I managed to stem the tide of tears and hysteria by the time I got to my office. I had actually worked until 3:30 p.m. before being sent home for blocking up the telephone lines for the entire building with my incessant calls to the day care.

Day three dawned. I thought I had the whole thing down pat. I dropped off my son, planted only thirty kisses on him before being forcibly ejected from the room and only cried to the first traffic light. I breezed into work and began my day.

Lunchtime came and went and still I hadn't dissolved into a puddle of tears. Apparently there was an office pool on how long I was going to last before being sent home. Having gone home early for the last two days, my breasts had not had time to get overfull, though as soon as I got my son and he latched on, they filled his mouth to overflowing. He took in what he could with the rest running down his little chin, soaking his shirt.

By 3 p.m. on day three, I still had not shown any signs of needing to leave, and my breasts were getting engorged and uncomfortable. Just as I was about to pop off to the bathroom to indulge in a bit of expressing (what fun! I could barely wait!), a client was shown into my section of the office. He began to talk earnestly about his need for new Web sites as I sat forward with my arms across my now aching breasts and rested my elbows on the top of the desk.

Unfortunately, just as he had launched into his most passionate speech yet, an ad came on the office radio, which included the sounds of a baby crying. Of course, as any lactating mother knows, this is a sound akin to the death knell for prison inmates.

My breasts splurged. There is no other word for what happened.

Suddenly, pools of milk appeared around my arms and began running down my shirt. Lurching backward only caused the milk to run faster, and as my shirt rapidly deteriorated to the consistency of a used, wet rag. My bewildered client did all he could to assure me his wife had had the same problem when she breastfed their children.

My male-dominated office dissolved into hysteria. I mumbled apologies and fled the scene.

When I came back to my desk half an hour later, dry, a cup size smaller and in a ratty sweatshirt borrowed from one of our part-time student employees, my desk was spotless.

But, there was a big pile of money and a sign that read, "Alright, you won the pool. You made 4 p.m. Go home and feed the baby."

Bad Mothering ...
or So I Thought

By Dorothy Thompson

I knew I should have paid attention when someone told me that being pregnant was the easy part and that it's what happens afterward that you had better be prepared for. Sometimes, it has to be a "been there, done that" experience to prove that theory correct. And even then, after all the abuse we suffer as a result, we roll over and do it again.

This is my true story of the joy, as well as the pain, of my experience as a new mother who thought she knew it all ...

"Congratulations!" the doctor told me. "You're pregnant!"

After eight months of trying to become pregnant, my dreams were finally becoming true: I was now blessed with a child and my husband and I would live happily ever after.

And then I woke up.

Reality had arrived at my doorstep, hitting me smack in the head on the way in. Now I was about to do something that I had never done before, and it scared the hell out of me.

I did what any baby-phobic person would do, and went to the library. I read everything I could on the subject. Dr. Spock became my soul mate. *Mr. Rodgers* and *Sesame Street* became my choices of viewing entertainment. I walked to the park and observed the mothers interact with their children as they wiped snotty little noses and refereed fights.

I became ENLIGHTENED.

I attended Lamaze classes, because that was the thing to do, and became knowledgeable in "natural childbirth."

Natural childbirth is equivalent to having all your teeth pulled without anesthesia or being run over by a Mack Truck, but they keep that a secret.

If everyone knew this, they would either a) never do it again, or b) stock up on every painkiller available and put the natural childbirth instructors out of business.

It May Be Natural, But It Ain't Easy

Nine months later to the day, it began.

Every few minutes, millions of electricity bolts shot through my body. Since I already had a prenatal appointment that day, I kept it, thinking the doctor would see me in excruciating pain and send me on to the hospital.

Wrong.

"I'm sorry, Ms. Thompson," she said. "You haven't dilated enough."

I followed orders and went back home.

When I thought I could take no more, I called the doctor back and told her I was going to the hospital. She sighed, knowing I'd be sitting there for hours in excruciating pain when I could be sitting at home in excruciating pain.

She was right.

Hours later, I could have been cast in *The Exorcist*. Not too long after that, THE DEMON HAD ARRIVED.

Melissa Nicole Thompson arrived screaming her lungs out, something she would continue the rest of her life. I lay there on the hospital bed, forgetting everything I had read about bonding with your infant. All I could think about was the pain I was enduring.

I couldn't sit, I couldn't walk, and after sixteen hours of labor, I was in no mood to bond with anyone. I must have missed the chapter on postpartum depression and my new child didn't let me forget it one minute.

I took my bundle of joy home and tried to nurse her. She screamed bloody murder all night long. Because I was going to try something completely alien to me called breastfeeding, I never bought a bottle. I wished that I had. I could have at least put water in it, if nothing else, to stifle her screams.

I paced back and forth, losing sleep and wishing I were dead. What was wrong with me? I had read everything about babies. Why was this happening to me?

The next day, my mother-in-law called. "How's the baby?" she asked.

"Uh ... wonderful ... she cried all night long," I told her.

Because my mother-in-law knew everything, which she had constantly reminded us the whole five years of our marriage, she suggested we come to her house. She would help us take care of baby, and I could get some much-needed rest.

I was exhausted and drained.

I gave in.

When we arrived, the force of grandmotherly wisdom set in. She grabbed the baby and I was instructed to go lie down. I relented and crawled under the blankets to recoup.

Every time the baby would cry, someone would pop their head in my door to see what the matter was. What is it about a boob hanging out that drives everyone to the scene?

Since I had read everything there was to know about breast-feeding, I knew that a) you had to be relaxed and b) you did not substitute formula for breast milk. Well-meaning grandmas must have missed that chapter.

I woke up in the middle of the night and my child was gone. I jumped out of bed and ran out into the living room where I saw my mother-in-law feeding a bottle of milk to my baby.

MY BABY.

Because she intimidated me, I just turned around, went back to bed and cried.

Needless to say, my milk dried up and never returned.

We went back home a week later, and no sooner than we had returned, the baby developed excruciating stomach pains. She screamed and I found myself wondering why I even had her.

I developed migraines, something I never had in my entire life, and found myself distancing myself from my husband, who never helped and always sided with my mother-in-law, knowing that I was indeed a bad mother.

Nursing a headache while my baby slept fitfully beside me, I was reading a parenting magazine. I peeked over at my newborn and guilt riddled me. She was so angelic, lying there in her sweet-smelling baby blankets. Tears welled in my eyes and I tossed the magazine aside. I turned over and the words on the back cover caught my eye: Does your baby experience gas? Does your baby cry endlessly and sleep fitfully? The ad was for a soybean-based formula for babies who were allergic to cow's milk.

I bolted straight up.

Could my baby be allergic to milk and I was not a bad mother after all?

I called my husband and told him to bring home some of this miracle milk.

For the first time in two weeks, my baby slept through the night and so did I.

A week later, I finally bonded with my new infant. Walking in the park became our solace and reunion. Our spirits intertwined with our souls and we become one.

And all it took was an ad in the back of a parenting magazine.

Nipple Woman

By Kathy Coudle King

Ouch! That really hurt!

I gently stuck my pinky finger between my nipple and my son's lips, unlatching him, then placed him back on, hoping this time we'd have it right. Ouch!

The kid had gums of steel and he was only a couple of weeks old. Scabs had formed on my nipples, and in the weeks ahead, scabs would form on top of the scabs. It even hurt having the cold air hit my nipples when I got out of the shower.

Ryan was my first child, and I had been looking forward to feeding him with my body. I had visions of myself as the Earth Mother, ready and able to feed my child whenever, wherever he wanted. I'd wear him in a sling across my stomach. No bottles to sterilize, no formula to mix. My husband, Alan, was all for nursing.

But that was before I almost lost a nipple.

Okay, I was probably never really in danger of losing a nipple, but I think I did raise a few eyebrows in the medical community. When I took Ryan in for his checkup a week after his birth, I mentioned to the pediatrician that I was extremely sore. I didn't say my nipples were sore because at this point I was so modest about my body that I could not even say the word "nipple."

So, I'm a little weird, but the doctor knew what I meant, especially when I began to unbutton my blouse. He began to blush and wave his hands.

"No, no! I'm not your doctor. You have to see your doctor if you're experiencing a problem."

Gosh, was I ever embarrassed.

So, I saw my doctor and he said, "No, no, you need to see your child's pediatrician."

Hmm … I figured I'd bring it up again at the next checkup. This was after I'd tried lanolin cream, frozen peas and chamomile tea bags on my nipples. I'd been flashing my husband and anyone who walked by our house in an attempt to air-dry after every feeding, of which there were many. My kid wanted to nurse every ninety minutes. I was not only exhausted but also convinced he was going to swallow one of my scabby nipples any day.

However, the pediatrician praised his weight gain. I mentioned that I was still feeling some soreness, and the pediatrician wrote down the name of a lactation consultant.

I left the clinic and walked right over to her office. She had a soothing voice, and cool hands, and asked if my son would nurse. Would he ever! We went into a private office with a sofa.

She began, "Have you tried the different positions?"

Like a good student, I quickly performed them. Yes. I seemed to be doing everything right. Six weeks was often the turning point. My baby was four weeks old. I could hang in there if it was only going to be two more weeks, I told myself.

Two more weeks and we'd be over the hump. But in the middle of the night, when you're experiencing acute sleep deprivation, two weeks can seem like forever. Tears were rolling down my cheeks at two in the morning.

Alan tried to reason with me, "Look, one bottle of formula will give you a rest and isn't going to do any harm."

The formula companies know that this night will come, so they send cases of formula. Now Alan wanted to use it. He couldn't bear to see me in pain, and what was one bottle?

"Fine," I said. "One bottle."

Alan practically ran out of the room, and the baby howled with hunger as I sat rocking him. I realize now that I put myself under unnecessary pressure. I'd gotten it in my head that I was going to nurse and, by golly, I was.

At this point, breast might have been best for my baby, but it wasn't doing me much good. Alan returned with the bottle, and when I tipped it back to Ryan's lips, liquid leaked all over. Both Ryan and I were drenched.

"Did you microwave it? You can't microwave the liner!" I shouted, and then with a gesture that is the marking of a true drama queen, I threw the bottle across the room. "Forget it! I'll feed my baby with my body!"

And I did, through the pain and the tears. I was never so miserable.

Then I saw it. It was an ad in the paper for the next La Leche meeting. I went. I went without my baby. Everyone else had a baby, some had two. But I left mine home. It was a breast-feeding meeting, and I left my baby home. Anyway, I mentioned I was having some soreness. I really wanted to show them my nipples, but I figured they might run out of the room before I could pump them for advice.

Well, not pump them exactly . . .

The leader told me I should go home and put vinegar on my nipples. If the soreness went away, chances were good the baby and I had thrush. This could easily be cured.

A cure?! I could hardly wait to get home.

I poured some vinegar in two soup bowls, placed them on the living room coffee table, and tore open my shirt and nursing bra. Into the soup bowls I stuffed my breasts while my frightened hubby looked on.

"Wh ... what are you doing, dear?" he asked.

"I'm giving my breasts a test," I answered, feeling the pain slowly fading.

"How are they doing?" he asked, one hand reaching for the phone to call the psych ward.

"Pretty good, I think," I said. Yes, this was it! The vinegar was doing the trick, and I was closer to solving this problem.

The next day I saw a nurse practitioner, explained my discovery, and she immediately pulled out a bottle of gentian violet. "Swab this on your nipples for a couple of days, and when Baby nurses he'll get some and soon the thrush will clear up."

It sounded so simple, and it was. I went home, got a cotton swab, and again sat in the living room and tore off my blouse. Again Alan watched in terror as I painted my nipples with the deep purple topical. I felt like an Amazon woman preparing for battle. I could accomplish anything I set my mind to. I stood up, hands on my hips and faced my frightened husband.

"Da-da-da-Da! It's Nipple Woman!" I took the baby, put him

It May Be Natural, But It Ain't Easy

on my purple nipple and only winced a bit.

By the end of the week the soreness was completely gone. My son and I truly became a nursing couple. I nursed him for twenty-two months, and I nursed my other three children for about as long. I totaled it up and together I fed babies with my breasts for a total of six and a half years. Not only can I now say nipple without blushing, but every other body part, body excretion and bodily function you can think of.

Would you expect any less from Nipple Woman?

Part Nine

The Unexpected Comes after the Expecting Is Over

It shot out across the room, across the line of consultants, over the tired mothers and the anxious fathers. It sprayed the filing cabinets on the other side of the room and it kept spraying for twenty minutes.

Out of Control

By Elizabeth L. Blair

Preboarding is a wonderful gift the airlines offer families with young children.

With car seats, diaper bags, bottles and blankets in hand, the parents shuffle down the Jetway to the confined space of an aircraft where they will spend the next few hours. Although the other passengers may feel a twinge of jealousy toward the lucky preboarders, they should actually be grateful that they are not in the same situation.

Flying with children is never an easy mission, at least not the first time. Nerves frayed, some parents give their children Benadryl in hopes that plugged ears don't become a problem. Other parents control the amount of caffeine their children ingest. Activities and DVD players are hauled along in hopes of entertaining the older ones. Of course, plastic bags full of cereal and emergency candy are always hidden inside the overstuffed diaper bag — just in case. As parents step on board, they cross their fingers and hope for the best. I've seen it a million times.

One particular Saturday, I was greeting the preboarding families in Baltimore as they folded their strollers before boarding the plane. We were on our way to Orlando, Florida, which usually means there will be a lot of kids on board. I helped by holding babies and warming up bottles.

One woman in particular was traveling alone. I took her purse and diaper bag as she carried her baby boy in the car seat. I helped her fasten the car seat into the seat by the window. She confided that this was her first trip flying as a mother. The baby was only ten weeks old. I told her that if she needed anything to just holler. I said that I would be happy to sit with her baby if she needed to use the restroom. She was very grateful.

During the safety demo, I explained that if the oxygen masks fell, to be sure and put it on herself first, then her baby. The woman nodded. Within a few minutes we were on our way to sunny Orlando.

Halfway through the flight, I was walking through the cabin with my white trash bag inquiring if anyone needed anything else. I heard a flight attendant call-light ding. I looked around the cabin. Spotting the light, I walked over. I looked at the three passengers sitting in the row. "Does someone need something here?" I asked.

The woman sitting on the aisle pointed toward the ceiling. "Something is leaking from one of the overhead bins. My book is all wet now." She held up her damp paperback romance novel.

Sure enough, there was some kind of liquid all over the ceiling. It wouldn't be the first time someone left a water bottle up there. I was inspecting the fluid, trying to determine where it was coming from, when I noticed a bald man sitting in the center seat two rows up, wiping his head with a cocktail napkin.

Confused, I opened the overhead bin, and peered in. It was dry. I moved forward to the next bin and as I popped it open, I looked down to see the new mom changing her baby's diaper.

The tray tables were soaked, as if a child had been having fun with a toy water gun. The mother looked up at me with guilty eyes and said, "I'm sorry. It got out of control." The baby squealed. "I would have taken him into the lavatory but the seatbelt sign is on."

I told her it was okay and went to retrieve some napkins from the galley to clean up the yellow mess. I handed the man sitting in front of her a napkin, then I wiped off the ceiling.

When I was just about done, the baby started to fuss, so his mom cradled him in her arms and lifted her shirt. The baby hushed for a minute as he suckled his mother's breast.

"Finally. I haven't been able to get him to nurse all morning since he's off his schedule. Maybe he'll fall asleep," she said.

Well, the baby certainly seemed to know what his mother had just said and he didn't like it. He threw back his head and let out a loud, unpleasant scream. Startled, the entire forward part of the cabin jumped.

As his mother caught her baby's head her breast milk kept flowing. The milk hit her baby in the face. When she tried to

The Unexpected Comes after the Expecting Is Over

reposition the breast, milk continued to spew, hitting the bald man's head.

I handed the man a clean napkin for a second time.

The milk continued to flow and the baby continued to scream. Getting him latched on again was impossible. The flow was too fast. The red-faced mother pulled down her shirt. With the show finally over, the baby quieted down and began searching for his mother's breast again. The mother lifted her shirt and tried again.

"What can I do for you?" I asked.

"After he is done feeding would you mind watching him while I change shirts?"

I hadn't seen her bring on a carry-on suitcase. "You have an extra shirt? That's good planning."

She flashed a weak smile. "Let's just say this isn't the first time this has happened. Sometimes it just gets out of control."

As for the bald gentleman, let's just say I arranged for him to get compensated for that flight. Fortunately, he was a good sport.

He was an ob-gyn.

Exhibit A

By Laura Irani

I am a lawyer. It's my job to be anal.

When I found out I was pregnant, I bought three books on breast feeding. I took a class. I researched breast pumps, breast pads, nursing bras, nursing pillows and nipple creams. I practiced holding a stuffed raccoon in proper nursing positions.

I was ready.

And my preparation paid off. After my son was born, breast-feeding went well, right up until the day I tested my double electric breast pump. I was actually excited to use it. For two months, I'd been nursing my baby with no idea how much milk he was getting. I couldn't wait to see those bottles fill up with all that good stuff I was making. So I read the pump instructions, boiled the plastic parts, air-dried the tubing, and settled down with a giant glass of water. And I watched as a tiny sprinkle of milk drops coated the bottom of the bottles.

Not even half an ounce.

I thought maybe I needed to get used to pumping. But I didn't get any more milk the second time I pumped, or the third, or the thirtieth.

A month before I was supposed to return to work, I panicked. My books said I should be pumping four ounces a day to get a good frozen milk reserve. I was lucky to get one or two ounces in a day. How would I manage when I returned to work full time?

I ate raw oatmeal. I drank dark beers. I took herbal supplements. No increase. And the last day of my maternity leave quickly approached.

I told myself things would get better once I was at work, pumping full time. My body would get used to it. I would produce more. But if I'd thought pumping at home was hard, pumping at work required Herculean effort.

I arrived at work my first day back with a sign to put on my office door during pumping sessions. I asked visitors to return in fifteen minutes. I thought this would allow me privacy to pump.

But it didn't.

I quickly learned there's no way to discreetly and professionally remove your clothing, hook yourself up to a machine and squirt milk from your breasts.

My books said to think about or look at pictures of my baby during pumping sessions to help the milk let down. But my books never told me that the important phone call I'd been waiting on for three days would always be returned mid-squirt. And they never mentioned how to answer the phone while pressing two plastic cones to your breasts. (The key is to squat in your chair, holding the cones in place with your thighs.)

And the mess! I may have pumped only a couple of ounces at a time, but somehow a carton ended up on my desk, my bra, my keyboard and any document within a two-foot radius of my desk. I kept a roll of paper towels in my desk drawer to wipe up the sprays of milk that resulted each time a cone slipped. (Slippage occurred two to three times a pumping session, given the unreliability of the thigh-hold method.) Thank goodness breast milk is white. I don't think my boss ever realized the damp, crinkly spots on the files were breast milk!

A month after my return to work, I was still struggling to pump enough milk for my son. Pumping sessions were hurried and uncomfortable. I constantly feared exposure. I kept my back to my office door. But I never bothered with the blinds. My office faced an empty wooded lot. And I was on the fourth floor. No one could see in.

One particularly busy morning, I frantically reviewed new IRS regulations while pumping. I used the thigh-hold while I pumped, so that I could flip pages with one hand and highlight with the other. I was so engrossed in my work that I failed to notice the noise from outside my office until it was too late.

There I sat — breasts exposed and oozing milk, squatting in my knee-length skirt with thighs separated and panties peeking through — face-to-face with the window washer.

He let out a yelp.

I let out a yelp.

I jumped for the blinds. Cones, bottles and milk splattered over the floor. I stood in my office for a few minutes, wondering if there was a professional way to handle this.

Would he tell anyone?

Would everyone laugh at me?

It took me almost an hour to calm down after the shock. I'm not sure how long it took the window washer. But after I recovered, I started to feel relief. The worst had happened. I'd been caught. The window washer had learned my secret: I'm a breastfeeding mom.

And I was still alive.

That afternoon, I pumped five ounces.

It was a record.

Night at the Opera

By Donna Conger

My first child would not nurse. Even in the hospital he got dehydrated because he wouldn't eat the sweet nectar my body had prepared for him, despite my best efforts.

So it was a joy when our second child, Celeste, arrived with a taste for my milk. It was an understatement to say that she was a good nurser.

Fifteen minutes after she was born, she latched onto me and didn't let go until she was weaned at seven months. If she wasn't eating, I was pumping milk into a bottle for those times out when nursing wasn't possible.

I was with her almost all the time. Her routine was demanding and I was exhausted after six weeks.

My husband saw this and, two months after she was born, announced that we were going out to dinner! And then, oh joy, he had somehow gotten tickets to Puccini!

I didn't especially love the opera, but I did a happy little dance anyway. A Saturday night out! I rushed to my closet. What to wear? I could wear silk! Or velvet! Anything that was dry-clean only, because there would be no baby spitting up or producing liquids from the other end.

I showered, fixed my hair and then sat down to nurse Celeste for a good long time before we left. I even left a bottle of pumped milk.

When I told my mother that there were a couple of bottles of milk in the freezer, she laughed, "Maybe this time, she won't paw my boobs."

She had fed Celeste once before, and we all had a good laugh when the baby turned away from the bottle of mother's milk and tried to nurse her grandmother.

As excited as I was, I hesitated after I picked up my cocktail purse and stared longingly at my chubby little milk-drinking machine.

"You two have a good time," Mom said, waving us out the door. "Don't worry about anything. We'll be fine!"

Nervous, but excited, we stepped outside, scrubbed, perfumed and child-free for the first time in months.

The night was magical. The waiter approached us about wine. I had read all of the books, but the euphoria of an evening out must have caused my brain to cease functioning, because we ordered a bottle of wine. During dinner, I drank half a bottle, and my husband drank the other half.

It never occurred to me that the wine would affect my milk flow.

Full and relaxed, we paid the bill and drove to the opera. I felt like a princess as the valet parked our car and we walked into the theatre. We held hands as we found our seats. We gazed into one another's eyes, and then read the program.

The lights went down. The orchestra struck up a tune. The singers made their entrance and exploded into song.

I listened intently, smiling and thinking how nice it was to sit and do nothing. I thought of our sweet little infant at home, and for a moment, I experienced a pang of concern. My mother was great, but could she handle the baby if she started to scream? What if she wouldn't eat?

What if ...

I tried not to think about Celeste, but my mind had locked onto the baby and it wouldn't let go. The song on stage was heart wrenching. A character was losing her child. My joy fell. I missed my baby. I would call home during intermission.

I felt a sudden swell in my breasts, the way I always felt just before feeding. Oh no, I thought. It's been three hours since she last ate! My breasts were used to giving up milk every three hours.

The tingling started and then my milk let down. In my excitement over an evening out, I had forgotten to put in my nursing pads.

The milk seeped through my silk blouse. Even in the dark, I could see ever-widening, wet circles as the milk quickly soaked through my bra, my slip, and then my blouse. It kept going until

The Unexpected Comes after the Expecting Is Over

it ran down my breasts. It started to make a puddle inside my bra. I could feel it squirting now. It was used to keeping up with the demand of a tiny, determined jaw, only there was no jaw, just an instinctive response.

I crossed my arms over my wet breasts, mortified. The singers stopped singing and left the stage to applause. The lights went up. Intermission! Oh, no!

I uncrossed my arms and tapped my husband on his shoulder.

"My milk," I said to my husband. "See?"

He tried to hide his amusement. I was not amused. Rivulets of milk seeped out of my bra and rolled down my stomach now.

"Did you bring a bottle?" he asked.

"Why would I do that?" I returned with a snap, as a pool of milk collected at the waistband of my skirt. "I need something to pump it into."

He thought for a moment. "Maybe there's a bottle in the car."

I shook my head.

"No?" he said.

"Why would I?"

The milk broke free of the waistband and started rolling down my stomach, past my hips.

"I gotta do something!"

I covered my chest with my wrap and sped out of the auditorium into the lobby.

"Look," my husband said. "Drinks."

"I'm not thirsty."

"No. We can buy a drink and you can pump the milk into the plastic cup."

"By hand?"

"Do you have a pump?" he asked with a grin.

I resisted the urge to slap him.

He was at the counter in a flash.

"Water, please," he ordered, while I pressed my legs together and prayed that the milk wouldn't drip onto the floor.

"We don't sell it," the clerk returned.

"Okay, I just need an empty cup."

"I have to sell you some soda."

"I don't want any soda!"

He ended up buying an empty plastic cup for five dollars. "I'll be in the bathroom," I said.

"No time. The lights are flashing. It'll be dark. You can do it during the opera."

It made sense. We scuttled back into the auditorium. I put the cup between my legs. The lights dimmed. I unbuttoned my blouse, hunched over, and milked my breasts. The screeching of the singers muted the sound of milk shooting into the cup. He giggled once or twice when he looked over to see me squeezing my breasts on each side and the milk squirting out with extreme force.

Fifteen minutes later, my breasts were empty and the twelve-ounce cup was half full. I held it up to my husband.

"Moo," he said.

I grinned.

And then swatted him.

Babies or Puppies, It Made No Difference

By Tenna Perry

On June 19, 1998, my daughter Catherine came into this world as a squirming, screaming, eight-pound, eight-ounce bundle of joy.

By the end of the next day, I was in the pits of depression because I felt I was the ultimate mothering failure. It seemed every female mammal in the world could breast feed her young except me.

It wasn't that I didn't try. It wasn't that the hospital's lactation consultant, Annie, hadn't put in overtime in her attempt to help me.

Annie looked at me for a minute and then asked, "Have you got anything against milking machines?"

"Huh?" My husband, David, and I asked in unison.

Laughing, Annie said, "Tenna, there are ALWAYS other options. It will just depend on how determined you are in feeding breast milk to Catherine."

An hour later, Annie had found me a double-barreled, electric milking machine (a.k.a. breast pump), a small, sterile bottle and nipple. Within minutes, Catherine was eagerly sucking down the rich, creamy milk.

In the weeks to come, I was shackled to that machine and my breasts were constantly confused as to the actual trigger for letdown. Was it the crying of a baby or the hiss of the automated pump?

Neither they nor I knew for sure.

While the hiss of the machine was a constant, it soon became apparent that the crying of any child, not just my own, was cause for milk flow. I never got through the local Wal-Mart with a dry shirt because hearing some other woman's child cry set my breasts into high gear.

When I went back to work in the veterinary clinic, I was under the misguided notion I wouldn't have to worry about leaking breasts again. I felt sure the milking breaks in the bathroom would be enough to keep things under control. It wasn't long before I realized the flaw in my thinking.

One Friday afternoon, a really gorgeous, thirty-year-old man came into the clinic with his boxer and her newborn puppies. As a happily married woman with a needy newborn at home, I was in no way interested in this man but couldn't help feeling an egotistical surge of womanliness as the boxer's owner and I spoke in the exam room and his interest in me became apparent.

I had never been shortchanged in the upper story, but after Catherine's birth, my breasts had taken on a whole new shape and had increased to such an amazing size that I had a difficult time fitting into the top of my surgical scrubs.

The Grand Canyon's depth had nothing on that of my cleavage.

Speaking to the client while examining the mother of the puppies, I went into my normal spiel concerning the nutritional needs of a lactating bitch, then I launched into symptoms of possible delivery complications to be on the lookout for over the next few days. All was going well until that first puppy began to feel lonely and started crying in his box.

I tried to ignore the tingling.

I leaned over the counter (giving the man a bird's-eye view down the front of my scrub top) and rested my chin on my cupped hands while I desperately pressed my forearms against my nipples in an attempt to stop the flow.

Soon though, a second and then a third puppy began crying. I tried to maintain a professional attitude and continue the discussion, but I knew all was lost when the man's eyes dropped from my cleavage to my scrub top and finally seemed to become fixated on the counter I was leaning over.

By this time, my breasts had become so large I couldn't even see the counter when I first looked down. I did see the wet spot that not only crossed my breasts but also reached each of my shoulders. Knowing full well that the burgundy color of my top matched the flush of embarrassment on my face, I stepped back from the counter and pulled the top far enough away from my belly to see the stain had reached all the way to the hem and on to my scrub bottoms. Put simply, I looked as if someone had doused the front of me with a bucket of water.

I glanced at the man who was still staring in amazement at the counter where, for the entire world to see, there was a puddle of my milk. Not knowing what to say or even if I should laugh or cry, I shut my eyes and shook my head. The focus of the man's eyes came back to my breasts as that small movement of my headshake brought forth the distinct "plip, plip, plip" sound of liquid hitting the hard tile of the exam room's floor.

Like a matched set of drippy faucets, my breasts were still pouring out the milk.

It was at that moment I decided that retreat was the better part of valor and literally ran from the exam room, through the waiting room full of people, to the seclusion of the bathroom with its ever-ready milking machine.

It was some twenty minutes later when the receptionist came knocking on the door to tell me the coast was clear. My emergence brought forth a peal of laughter from both the receptionist and the doctor on duty.

Thankfully, the doctor was a father of five and mercifully gave me permission to go home early.

If It Moves, Nurse It

By Peggy Vincent

Colin was my first baby, and he taught me everything I needed to know about breastfeeding. But one night when he was four months old, somewhere around 2 a.m., he just wouldn't cooperate.

I always tucked Colin into bed between my husband and me to nurse him during the night, and sometimes, of course, we both fell asleep afterward and slept on till it was time for the next feeding a few hours later.

On this particular night, I heard his snuffling, baby-animal noises, felt him squirming next to me, and then he began rooting at my chest. Still three-quarters asleep, I unbuttoned my nightgown and pulled him toward me. But he wouldn't latch on, a highly unusual behavior for The Olympian Nurser.

As I tugged him closer, I noticed he had somehow wiggled out of most of his clothes. Figuring he must just be cold, and maybe that's why he wouldn't suck, I wrapped an edge of my flannel nightgown around him, tucked my sheet and blanket snug around his struggling body and repositioned him once more.

Still Colin wouldn't nurse.

I rubbed his back, whispered into his ear, stroked his bald little head and guided my nipple toward where I knew his mouth must be. He had always had the ability to find my nipple, even in pitch darkness. It was as if he had a radar system operating, so I couldn't understand his sudden ineptitude.

Then my husband's voice came from somewhere off to my left. "Peggy, stop. Stop, already. What on earth are you trying to do to my arm?"

Arm?

I blinked, awakened fully and saw my husband's incredulous face as he tried to free his arm from my tenacious grasp. I had swaddled his bare arm multiple times in the folds of my

The Unexpected Comes after the Expecting Is Over

blue-flowered nightgown, and in the sheets and blankets. I had rubbed his forearm, stroked his bicep and whispered into the crook of his arm.

And, with dogged determination, I had tried to breastfeed his elbow.

Colin, just beginning to make those little night sounds of a baby who's getting hungry, lay in his crib across the room.

The Dancers Really Sucked

By Susan Hines

The chicklets, Abby and Kelly, were eight months old. We were old hands at this nursing thing — we had it down to a science! I didn't plan for the twin meltdown that occurred that day.

The girls had just awakened from their naps. As usual, I turned on their "wake up" music — some Raffi stuff that made them giggle and smile while they took turns with diaper changes. I finished changing Kelly, turned around and put her in Abby's bed. Picked up Abby to change her diaper, and Kelly started making the American Sign Language sign for "milk." Oops. Guess the diaper changes were taking a little too long. By the time I got started changing Abby's diaper, she, too, was making little sounds of frustration.

I finished Abby's diaper and went back to her bed to collect her twin. Abby was NOT happy to be put down for even one second. She immediately clutched part of my nursing shirt in her left fist and started sucking her thumb while crying. Kelly just stood crying at the rail of the crib and did her "tongue thing" and signed "milk" repeatedly.

Need I mention that I was becoming VERY engorged?

All of the sudden, it occurred to me, "they're the perfect height!" I made a little glance backward — yes, the blinds were open, but my back would be to the window and no one could see what I'd be doing. I immediately flipped up the top of my nursing shirt, flipped down the flaps of my nursing bra, and the girls attacked!

Ahhhh, relief. And it was so easy!

No, not so easy.

I had forgotten about the Raffi music playing on the radio. My beautiful little girls noticed. And started "dancing."

Yes, dancing while nursing. It's a moment I'll never forget.

Just call me "Bessie."

The Explosion

By Theresa Kane

A house with a newborn can be a crazy, busy place. When the infant first comes home, your complete focus is on that baby's care — and other things like your social life don't rate at all.

If showers barely rate, how can a social life hope for attention?

Three months after our second born, Justin, arrived, the time had come for me to reclaim a little piece of my life, outside my role as a mother. An invitation to two parties seemed like a wonderful reintroduction to adult life.

A Sunday brunch, followed by an elegant afternoon tea. How lovely! This was more adult company than I had had in months!

In hindsight, it does seem like an ambitious plan, even for a confident, experienced nursing mom. It was also a lot of social activity for him. Cute as a button and good-natured, he was the center of attention at both parties. Who could resist that smile and those big, blue eyes? His round cheeks, at both ends, got pinched — and he soaked in the love.

One party was joy for this milk-drunk child, but a second was too much. He grew tired of the attention and did as all overwhelmed babies have done before him. He sought comfort at my breast. He nursed and nursed and nursed and nursed, and then when he was done, he nursed some more.

Monday arrived and Justin caught up on his sleep. Now babies like routine, and it turns out that breasts like routine too. On Sunday, they had been given the signal by Justin that he was really, really hungry. Monday, there was a different signal. Frankly, they were confused. The extra nursing on Sunday meant that my breasts thought it was time to increase their milk production. The extra sleeping on Monday meant that there was nowhere for that extra milk to go.

Milk? Less milk? More milk? What do we do? What do we do?

By Tuesday, for a deceptive few hours, things seemed to be back to normal. Justin nursed on schedule, but before too long, the whole thing wasn't working: Justin was crying and cranky. And, my breasts were surprisingly full. The milk didn't seem to have anywhere to go and Justin couldn't be satisfied.

Now, even confident nursing-pro moms can panic and I am no exception. I pulled out all my books. I scrounged for the training notes. I called friends and applied every breastfeeding technique that I had ever heard of, from hot compresses and even hotter showers, to cabbage leaves and the dreaded nipple manipulation.

NOTHING worked.

By Wednesday morning, my breasts were the size of two large melons and as a hard as granite. The right one, Justin's personal favorite, seemed to stand at attention. Was it an infection? Was the baby sick? Had the milk turned to shakes that were stuck in the tubes? The quick call to the experts at a hotline confirmed the obvious: It was time to get some serious help! So, Justin and I headed off to the clinic, trying desperately to keep up with my breasts.

At the clinic, we took our seats among the many new moms who were learning how to nurse for the first time. They gently held what seemed, in comparison, to be tiny newborns. They tentatively uncovered their breasts and the lactation consultant took them through the basics. It was a calm, reassuring atmosphere — the ideal place to nourish and bond with your child.

Then, there was us.

The lactation consultant took one look at my super-sized breasts. The "tut-tut-tut" that she muttered gave me some clue that this was serious business. The verdict was clear.

"You have blocked ducts. The white specks here are not an infection. They are dried milk. All we have to do it 'flick' this off and the milk will start flowing. Let me get my 'tool' to take care of this."

Ours, apparently, was a case of exceptional educational value. "Would you mind if I call in some of the consultants-in-training?" asked the consultant. "We haven't had a case like this

The Unexpected Comes after the Expecting Is Over

in a long time."

"Sure, that's fine with me," I replied. (Anything to get those breasts flowing again was fine by me.)

One person in a lab coat entered this already crowded room.

Then a second... and a third....

There were others lined up outside who couldn't get in. And the parents of newborns all gathered around, anxious to learn a trick or two that might help down the road. I tried not to be embarrassed. Desperation, I've discovered, can often be a handy mask for embarrassment.

The consultant took her "tool," and flicked at the dry milk spot — and it started. Milk didn't leak out. It didn't flow out. It didn't flush out.

It shot out.

It shot out across the room, across the line of consultants, over the tired mothers and the anxious fathers. It sprayed the filing cabinets on the other side of the room, and it kept spraying for twenty minutes.

Justin was called into action. What better way to use breast milk than to give it to the hungry child?

Now breast milk is a good thing, but there can also be too much of a good thing. He sputtered. He spat and he couldn't keep up. Instead, we taped a bottle liner on each breast and watched three bottles of milk spray from my breasts. Then, and only then, was Justin ready to take up the challenge and finish the job he had started.

If he grows up with a fear of fountains, I should be able to explain it to him.

Part Ten

From the Other Side
of the Stirrups

*Fathers don't get much credit for
what we go through dealing with the
delivery of a child. We're about as
important as the movie extra in the
third row of the crowd scene in
Godzilla.*

Dads in the Delivery Room

By Charles Dowdy

Pregnant women have lured their husbands into the labor and delivery room. Why is it important that we be there? Is it because of the inspiration we men, who have no concept of such torture, can provide while women try to push that thing out? Or is it to give our lovely wives someone toward whom they can channel their hate as they labor through the excruciating pain?

No, they only want us there so we may witness this ordeal, so that we may view their great effort. Why would this be important?

Simple. So we'll change more diapers once the child is born.

Stay with me here.

To prepare for the delivery, we must attend totally unnecessary childbirth classes where we will have entire classes dedicated to breathing. Are we stupid to fall for this? The wife's only been breathing her whole life — suddenly we're required to count for her?

In addition to counting for a grown woman, another very important duty for us is changing the New Age CD being played to provide a relaxing atmosphere in that sterile, cold hospital room where she's wearing a paper gown and preparing to hike her legs up in stirrups.

I know you're thinking to yourself: What portable CD player? What New Age music? To this day, I do not know what New Age music means.

I do recall my wife screaming, "Turn that New Age junk off!"

These delightful melodies will be on the list you will get in childbirth class. This list is a collection of things you will HAVE TO HAVE in the delivery room.

In addition to New Age music, we also HAD TO HAVE candles. (I think it is always a good policy to have an open flame with canisters of oxygen lying around.) And we HAD TO HAVE a tennis ball. In theory, she was supposed to squeeze it. In reality, she threw it at my head.

Thank God we didn't HAVE TO HAVE a bowling ball.

Let me tell you that the things on this list do not help. If you want to put it in the male perspective, having a baby would be like trying to pass the mother of all kidney stones and thinking that sitting around in our underwear while watching ESPN and eating pork rinds might somehow make it a more pleasant experience.

Oh, and the film: Find out when you're supposed to watch the childbirth video and, by all means, MISS THIS SESSION! Childbirth is gross enough, and this ain't a Playboy Playmate having that baby.

Now a man might ask himself, "Why would she actually want me in there for her labor and delivery? I can barely remember to feed the dog, and she's thinking I'll be able to help with this child? Or does she want me there because birth is beautiful?"

What delivery did these people watch?

Look at it this way: When I change a dirty diaper, I announce to the world how rancid the thing is, even if it isn't, because I want credit for the dirty diaper change.

If I don't seek this credit, then I hear, "Since that last one wasn't so bad, will you change this one too?"

But if I make the last stinker seem like a combination of Chernobyl and three-year-old potato salad, then I get time off for good behavior when the next one smells around.

Women employ this theory on the front end before the kid is even born. If you are already enrolled in the childbirth class, then you've fallen into a trap. By your very unnecessary participation in the delivery room, you will witness her pain and, unless you are a total weasel, will be forced to help with the child simply out of guilt.

If you have completed your childbirth course, there is only one opportunity left.

Wait for the first contraction and start running around the delivery room, pulling your hair and screaming, "The Germans are coming" until the hospital staff is forced to sedate you. This is the only way you can help yourself.

Unless the kid comes out looking like your third cousin, Ed, then the dirty diapers will be his problem.

It's No Walk in the Park
for the Pregnant Father Either

By Gordon Kirkland

Whenever I write about pregnancy and childbirth, I can usually expect a flood of letters from outraged readers who don't have the same point of view about the entire process. Okay, I admit it, my take on the topic is clouded by the fact that I am a father, not a mother. I'm the guy who is supposed to stand in the corner and try not to get in the way by passing out at the sight of afterbirth.

Husbands just don't get it.

I don't think we are even supposed to get it.

It's probably best if we just go along for the ride and try to stay out of our wives' arms reach for most of the first two trimesters and definitely for all of the third. We should take the nausea, mood swings and cravings in stride. If at all possible, we should do our utmost to avoid causing any of the nausea or cravings and, assuming that we are not suicidal, we should avoid even mentioning the mood swings.

I always thought the odd cravings were just something that situation comedy writers used to get a laugh. Little did I know that when my wife decided that she wanted mushrooms at 10 p.m. that I should be expected to somehow produce a plate full of mushrooms for her late-night dining pleasure.

I should mention that we lived in the country, thirty miles from the nearest store. When my incredulous response seemed to be leading up to one of those aforementioned mood swings, I decided that it might be prudent to go out and buy some mushrooms. I was relieved to find that the one convenience store still open at that hour had a can of sliced mushrooms.

I just knew I'd be a hero on my triumphant return home.

Oh, how wrong a husband can be.

Even at the best of times, I know that if a husband speaks in the forest and there is no one there to hear him, he will still be wrong. Bringing home canned mushrooms to an expectant mother who was expecting her husband to return with fresh mushrooms is not just wrong. It's a surefire way to set off a mood swing of epic proportions.

Assuming that we survive the entire pregnancy, we are then faced with the fraud that is perpetrated upon us by doctors and prenatal class instructors who do their level best to convince people that the birth of a child is a simple, straightforward and enjoyable procedure. Let's face it folks, these people have a significant conflict of interest. Their incomes are maintained by people who can be convinced that giving birth is a beautiful thing.

Beautiful?

Exciting maybe. Perhaps awe inspiring. I'll even go as far as euphoric. But beautiful ... I don't think so.

The whole thing looked like someone trying to squeeze an angry wet cat through a hole in a balloon.

Of course, I realize that everyone's experience is unique. We always hear about those people who wake up on their due date, realize they are in labor, decide to rewallpaper the nursery, bake a couple of loaves of bread, drive themselves to the hospital and an hour later painlessly give birth to a set of twins.

We also hear about tooth fairies, flying reindeer and effective members of the senate.

Both my sons wanted to stay in the warm comfort of their private wombs for as long as possible. The oldest resisted the forces of Diane's organized labor for a full forty-three hours. The second one found a way to prevent labor from even starting until a full three weeks after he was scheduled to make his appearance. After thirty-eight hours of labor, he came into the world by cesarean section. He still has no concept of time. It does, however, explain the boys' fondness for pizza.

One was delivered and the other was take-out.

Fathers don't get much credit for what we go through dealing with the delivery of a child. We're about as important as the movie extra in the third row of the crowd scene in *Godzilla*. We're there, we're needed to make the scene complete, and there is a screaming monster threatening to do bodily harm if she can get her hands on us, but you're not going to hear a word about our importance to the production in the reviews.

Women talk about the agony they had to endure to give life to their offspring. No one cares about the agony of the father. I tried holding my wife's hand in the delivery room. When a contraction hit, I thought my hand had been run over by a bus. Professional wrestlers could never hope to develop a grip like that. When I finally managed to free my hand, another contraction kicked in, and she grabbed my arm. I still have an outline of her fingernails clearly visible on my upper arm.

Did any of the medical staff think to offer me an epidural? Of course not, I'm just the father.

I firmly believe that letting fathers into the delivery room is the single greatest reason the postwar baby boom ended. We went through the first twenty years after the Second World War with babies popping out all over. In the late sixties and early seventies, when fathers started staying with their wives instead of going outside where it's safe, the birthrate dropped faster than you can say, "You want me to do WHAT to the umbilical cord?!?!"

If the governments of Third World countries want to slow their population growth, they should just start insisting that fathers go into the labor rooms. It'll be more effective than all the birth-control programs put together.

I know it worked for me.

When we arrived at the hospital prior to the birth of our youngest son, I stayed behind filling out forms, while Diane was taken ahead to the maternity ward. I was understandably concerned for her well-being and secretly even more concerned for my own. After all, it had only been two-and-a-half years since our first child, and the memories of the pain I went through that time were still fresh in my mind. I was also trying to remember those breathing exercises that we learned in prenatal class the first time around. I didn't want anyone hyperventilating and passing out onto the incubator. After the last time, I know just how upset nurses get when the fathers do that sort of thing.

From the Other Side of the Stirrups

Sensing my apprehension, the nurse tried to get me talking. "Is this your first?" she asked.

"No," I replied, "This is my last ... definitely my last."

Meet the Contributors

*She is proud to admit that this is the
first time she has written about using
the bathroom in public. She's just
not sure whether to include it in
her portfolio.*

Meet the Contributors

Penny Aicardi
Dead Serious

Penny Aicardi is a sportswriter who resides with her husband, John, in Whitinsville, Massachusetts. Ms. Aicardi currently serves as the NASCAR Busch North Series columnist and editor at *Speedway Scene*, an auto racing trade publication in the Northeast. She's the mother of two: Samantha (5) and Jason (9 months).

Christine Allen-Riley
Confessions of a Seatbelt Zealot

Christine Allen-Riley has given birth only twice, but she cares for up to seven day-care children. Despite this, she continues to be a romantic at heart and is pursuing a career as a romance novelist. She resides in Grand Rapids, Michigan with her husband, Matt, their two young sons, Killian and Corwin, and seven neurotic cats. These days, she drives her own car. Her brother's car has limped along to the Parking Garage of the Great Beyond (lot 666), where it belongs.

Jan Andersen
I'm Not Too Old!

Jan Andersen is a freelance writer and copywriter, with twenty-one years' marketing and PR experience. In addition to writing commercial copy for a broad spectrum of audiences, Jan specializes in compelling articles and features on diverse lifestyle topics and social issues. She has also participated in many TV and radio programs. Jan also owns and runs five Web sites: World Writer, Mothers Over 40, Child Suicide, SACS (Surviving After Child Suicide) and Jan Andersen Writing Services. Until recently, Jan had four children aged 20, 17, 16 and 4. Her eldest son, Kristian, tragically took his own life on November 1, 2002. While campaigning for depression, suicide and drugs awareness, Jan is writing a book on child suicide entitled *Chasing Death*.

Elizabeth L. Blair
Out of Control

Elizabeth L. Blair resides in Arizona with her husband and two stepsons. She is anxiously awaiting the birth of her first baby, due in June 2004. Elizabeth works as both a freelance writer and flight attendant. Her work has appeared or been accepted for publication in many online and print publications such as the *Christian Science Monitor*, *The Dollar Stretcher*, *Chicken Soup for the Bride's Soul*, *Chocolate for the Woman's Soul* (sequel), and many more. Currently, she is working on her first book, tales of her humorous journeys in the airline industry.

Jackie Buxton
What They Don't Tell You about the Time To Push

After graduating in 1992, Jackie Buxton worked in public relations for charities. But her heart was in fiction, so when her job was declared redundant two weeks before her wedding, she felt that something was telling her to ditch the day job and write her novel. Five years and two wonderful daughters later, the novel is being submitted. Meanwhile, she writes anything and everything to keep the bread and butter coming in. But she is proud to admit that this is the first time she has written about using the bathroom in public. She's just not sure whether to include it in her portfolio.

Donna Conger
Night at the Opera

Donna Conger was born and raised in Junction City, Kansas. She left at age eighteen to attend college in Massachusetts, where she met her first husband and the father of the child in her story. Donna currently lives in Utah with her second husband, four children and two dogs, and together they raise purebred beagles. Donna is the published author of four romantic suspense novels, one nonfiction book and over one hundred poems, short stories and articles. Her daughter Celeste is now eighteen years old and is employed as a full-time sales person, part-time model and actress.

S. (Shae) A. Cooke
My Milk-Depot Years

Shae Cooke is a mother, inspirational writer, domestic humorist and former foster child. A writer for all reasons and seasons, Shae shares her heart with a worldwide audience. She lives in beautiful British Columbia with her family and a host of misfit animals — a miniature parrot with a big attitude, a one-legged frog, a cross-eyed gerbil, two neurotic cats, an aged but beloved black Labrador retriever and Dick the beetle, buried somewhere amid a sea of manuscripts on her desk.

Tami Crea
The Toes Are Supposed to Be There, Doctor

Tami Crea is a mom to two boys, a writer, a graphic designer and a publisher. She runs an e-newsletter filled with activities for parents of preschool children called *Preschool Play*.

Meet the Contributors

Barbara David
False Labor Pains a Real Pain
Barbara David lives in Cincinnati, Ohio, with her husband, Geoff, and their five children. She earned a Phi Beta Kappa key during her undergraduate studies and taught English, journalism and film studies before becoming a stay-at-home mom. Barbara enjoys freelance writing in moments between helping with homework and changing diapers.

Charles Dowdy
Dads in the Delivery Room
Charles Dowdy manages a small cluster of radio stations in Louisiana and Mississippi. Married seven years, he and his wife have four children under the age of six. Charles writes a weekly newspaper column about his family, sharing the trials and triumphs of a sometimes wild and always abundant fatherhood.

Amanda Euringer
No Small Potatoes
Amanda Euringer has been an actor, director, janitor, house-painter, dog walker, teacher, condom seller, face painter, bartender, as well as a mother to large dogs, children and numerous well-behaved houseplants (though not necessarily in that order). Amanda completed her bachelor of fine arts in theatre — with a specialization in dramaturgy. She interned at the Playwrights' Workshop in Montreal. After several years of working on new Canadian plays and many adaptations of Shakespeare, Amanda moved to the Canada's west coast to pursue her love of theatre in a warmer climate. Although Amanda has worked in the field of language and storytelling all her life, this is her first published story.

Cheryl Fury
The Skinny on Pregnancy
Dr. Cheryl Fury lives in Saint John, New Brunswick, Canada with her husband and two young sons. She teaches history at the University of New Brunswick and St. Stephens University. Her area of specialization is the social history of Elizabethan seafarers and she's published academic articles and a book in this field. In her spare time, she plays soccer, plays bass guitar in a rock band and writes for fun.

Cindy Graul

Afternoon Sickness

Cindy Graul lives in Wyncote, Pennsylvania with her husband, Bert, and her three children: Allison (7), Alex (5) and Bradley (4). She has a professional photo business that she runs in her spare time producing casual portrait photography. This is Cindy's first publication. She had planned to have four kids over the course of sixteen years, but managed instead to produce three in three years and survived a total of twenty-seven LONG months of full-day sickness! WHEW!

Sheri Guyse

Girl Interrupted

Sheri Guyse, a freelance writer, resides in Oklahoma City with her daughter and husband. Thankfully, he was not permanently scarred by the operatic emissions of her pregnant body. Sheri's writing regularly appears in such prestigious places as the backs of receipts, Happy Meal napkins and her checkbook register. When Sheri isn't scrambling for a moment to complete a thought, she and her two-year-old watch *The Wiggles* and dance together.

She says, "I considered myself well-versed on what to expect. How clueless I was!"

Megan Kelley Hall

The Ten Biggest, Fattest Pregnancy Lies Exposed

Megan Kelley Hall is a freelance writer based in Marblehead, Massachusetts. She has written on parenting, health and fitness, and lifestyle issues for national publications including *Boston Magazine*, *Working Mother*, *American Baby*, and the *AKC Gazette*. She learned quickly about pregnancy surprises after giving birth to her first child three months early due to placenta previa. Piper Elizabeth, born at 2.5 pounds, is now a healthy and beautiful toddler who is constantly discovering new ways to distract her mother from her writing. Megan is currently working on her first novel.

Virginia Heffernan

Well, Officer, It's Like This …

Virginia Heffernan is a former geologist and principal of GeoPen Communications, a research and writing service for the resource and environmental sectors. The youngest of eight, she lives in Toronto with her husband, Roger, an exploration geologist, and her son, Graham. Neither Virginia nor Graham has had any more run-ins with police since that hot day in July.

Meet the Contributors

Dorothea Helms
Call a Pain a Pain

Dorothea Helms is a freelancer writer, editor and writing instructor who lives in Sunderland, Ontario, Canada. Dorothea's work, much of it humor, has appeared in publications across North America, and she has been featured twice on CBC Radio's *First Person Singular*. She has poked fun at her family in print since 1993 (hey, it's a living!). As of 2003, she has been married for thirty-two years. Her son is twenty-eight years old, married and living in Raleigh. Her daughter is twenty-one and is studying art history at the University of Toronto. Dorothea is also a published poet and aspiring novelist.

Kirsten Hines
Kegal-Woman
A Visit from the Titty Fairy

Kirsten Hines is a wife and mother of two. Jack, who is three, and Katherine, eighteen months. She freelances in her spare time while working at the Springfield YMCA in New Jersey as the membership director. You can read her work in such publications as the *Philosophical Mother* online magazine.

Susan Hines
The Dancers Really Sucked

Susan Hines and her military husband, Steve, and their five-year-old twin girls live in Indianapolis. Susan is a never-at-home stay-at-home mom, active in Girl Scouts, Southside Parents of Multiples and "preserving my sanity as much as possible."

Laura Irani
Exhibit A

Laura Irani lives in Austin, Texas with her husband, Ted, and son, Vincent. Laura works part time as an attorney and as a freelance writer. Laura specializes in employee benefits law.

Kate M. Jackson
The Pen

Kate M. Jackson is a freelance writer and mom who misplaces her shoes and keys at least twice a day. Her true passions include hanging out at the beach — off-season — with her family, reading "thinking-women's trash," and snuggling with her iPod. She spends her free time bidding on handbags on eBay and making up songs to sing to her daughter. Greatest hits include: *The Clean Bum Club* and *Beautiful Baby with a Big Buddha Belly*. She lives in Boston with her husband, James, her daughter, Caroline, and a portly pug named Vito.

Melinda Jones
My Dad's Delivery
Melinda Jones was born and raised in Oregon and is a graduate of Oregon State University. She currently lives in Connecticut with her husband, who is a member of the United States Navy, and their two children. Melinda is a freelance writer and a stay-at-home mom.

Theresa Kane
The Explosion
Theresa Kane is an entrepreneur who specializes in communications. Humor is now the most recent genre added to her writing portfolio. Whether in her role as founder of Viva Voce Press Inc., consulting with clients or cajoling her two young sons, Matthew and Justin, Theresa tries to live in that gap between expectations and reality. When she doesn't find it, it has a habit of finding her.

Candy Killion
This Ain't My First Time Around, Doc
Candy Killion is a freelance writer, mother of four and grandmother of two, whose wit has appeared in numerous greeting cards, northeastern US newspapers and magazines, and trade publications. Newly transplanted to Florida, she does her best work on the Fort Lauderdale beach, holding a glass with one of those funny little umbrellas. The product of her second labor, chronicled here, is twenty-year-old Chris. He is a smart aleck like his mother.

Kathy Coudle King
Nipple Woman
Kathy Coudle King writes essays, plays, screenplays, and had her first novel, *Wannabe*, published in 2000. In the early nineties, she was the playwright-in-residence at the University of North Dakota Women's Center, where she wrote plays about women's friendship, eating disorders and domestic abuse. Currently, she lives in Grand Forks, North Dakota, where she teaches writing and women's studies. She and her husband are raising four children, ages three to nine. She collects stories about "firsts" in women's lives and publishes them on her Web site.

Meet the Contributors

Gordon Kirkland
It's No Walk in the Park for the Pregnant Father Either

Gordon Kirkland is an award-winning author and syndicated columnist. His first book, *Justice Is Blind – And Her Dog Just Peed In My Cornflakes*, received Canada's Stephen Leacock Award of Merit for Humour in 2000. His latest book, *Never Stand Behind A Loaded Horse* is another collection of his stories, which focus on life from the perspective of a husband and father rapidly approaching the half-century mark. His frequent live TV and radio appearances in both Canada and the United States bring his stories to an ever-increasing and appreciative audience. He is the senior editor at Viva Voce Press Inc.

Anita Kugelstadt
Confessions of a Knocked-Up Knucklehead

Anita Kugelstadt lives with her three children and partner, Pierre, in Quebec City, Canada. She has worked as a teacher, waitress, chambermaid, curriculum designer and cook — all of which were perfect training for motherhood. She is currently working on her first novel.

Abby Lederman
Egg

Abby Lederman, mother of firstborn "Egg" and twins three years younger, is coauthor with Dr. Jeff Kaplan of the book *Finding The Path: A Novel for Parents of Teenagers*. She and Dr. Kaplan run teleclasses and coach parents of teens from their Web site at www.parenting-teenagers-today.com. They are the co-founders of "Love-A-Teen Day," a celebration acknowledging the struggle, joy and triumph of today's teens.

Heather Lodge
My Boobs Hurt

Heather Lodge is a freelance humor and fiction writer living in southwestern Pennsylvania. She has been employed both as a technical writer and as a proofreader/editor, and is currently enjoying her newest professional challenge: motherhood.

Christy Lui
Confessions of an Earth Mother Dropout

Christy Lui is most inspired when her expectations for being a mother clash with reality, which is often daily. Instead of getting depressed, she gets even. Her most thrilling writing moments are when someone reads her work and says thank you for being brave enough to say what I wish I could say. Her work has appeared in *Brain, Child* magazine, *SASS* magazine, *metroparent* Wisconsin, other regional parenting publications, and online at mommytales.com. She lives with husband John, sons TJ (5) and Ben (3), two fish — Flippy and Sticky, and Gazoo, the psycho-kitten, in Dousman, Wisconsin.

Nadine Meeker
Wheelman
Nadine Meeker is a freelance writer, editor and journalist of fifteen years residing in Michigan with her husband, daughter and a menagerie of pets. She is also a screenwriter and producer with NiteOwl Productions. Her first novel, *Pennsylvania Avenue*, is set for release in 2004 with Baycrest Books. In her spare time, she enjoys motorcycling, painting and campy television shows.

Christine Miles
In the Middle of the Night
Christine Miles is the mother of three busy children — Braden, Nikki and Liam. She is a stay-at-home-during-the-day-mom, and works in a busy doctor's surgery as a registered nurse two evenings a week. Christine enjoys baking, walking, playing and reading. She lives with her husband, Derek, and children in Auckland, New Zealand.

Jennifer D. Munro
Half Mast
Jennifer D. Munro's stories about fertility issues have appeared in *Calyx, Kalliope, Room of One's Own, Clean Sheets* and *Slow Trains*. She was a Hedgebrook resident, an Artist Trust grant recipient and the Seattle Writers Association's essay contest winner.

Lisa Nicholl
Evening Shoes
Lisa Nicholl had some good practice at resting while expecting her daughter Olivia. Olivia, on the other hand, used that time in utero to store up her energy for the many activities that showcase her talents today. From singing to dancing to writing stories, Olivia rests when she is sleeping and now Mom does, too. When not with Olivia, Lisa is the creative talent and business visionary that steers a home-decorating chain to success. Evening Shoes is her first published short story.

Meet the Contributors

Jamie M. Pearson
A Breastfeeding Annual Report
Jamie Pearson, whose writing has recently appeared in *Brain, Child* magazine, at imperfectparent.com, and in *Toddler: Real-Life Stories of Those Fickle, Irrational, Urgent, Tiny People We Love*, came to writing circuitously via a degree in political science and a career selling bonds on Wall Street (an odd job for her as she is both highly principled and bad at math). She currently lives in London, England with her husband, Rich, four-year-old daughter Avery and eighteen-month-old son Max, and is at work on a book about the misadventures of expatriate parenting.

Tenna Perry
Babies or Puppies, It Made No Difference
Tenna Perry is a native Texan who lives happily in the country with her husband, three children, five collies, a snobbish cat and one temperamental hedgehog. She holds black belts in both Bushido Kai and American Freestyle Karate. With her husband, Tenna has taught karate, self-defense and rape prevention for ten years. In addition to her martial arts background, Tenna has more than thirteen years' experience in small animal veterinary medicine and seven years in equine medicine. She is also a survivor of child sexual abuse and rape with extensive writings online concerning all of the subjects mentioned above.

Irene A. Pileggi
Express Delivery
Irene Pileggi is a mother of three beautiful girls — Alexis, Allie and Brooke. She currently is a stay-at-home mom who decided to take a break from the corporate environment and enjoy being with the kids. Irene likes writing, reading and spending the most time possible with her family. They currently live in Westchester County, New York. Irene has a certificate in computer arts and an associate's in business administration.

Tamara Talbot
My Perfect Plan for a Perfect Birth
Tamara Talbot is a mother, creative director and all-around do-it-on-paper lover. Her patient education materials have been proven to help sufferers of various diseases including COPD and Asthma. Her most challenging communications project yet is in raising two girls, Karley and Devan, with her extremely patient husband, Todd.

Her ultimate goal in life is to help her girls follow their dreams and to build on their talents. Piece of cake!

Dorothy Thompson
Bad Mothering … Or So I Thought
Dorothy Thompson is a freelance writer, author, editor, journalist and anthologist from the eastern shore of Virginia. She has written for many publications, as well as her online writing site, The Writer's Life www.thewriterslife.net, one of *Writer's Digest* magazine's Top 101 Web sites. She is the author of a children's book, *No More Gooseberry Pie*, and is the founder of the *Romancing the Soul* series of anthologies. Dorothy is also editor of the online humor column, *"Where's The Damn Picket Fence"*? She lives with her three children, Melissa, Ryan, Amanda Jane and her three dogs, Cassie, Max and Skylar.

Grace Tierney
What Blooming Really Means
Grace Tierney is a freelance writer who lives in Ireland and whose first child, Daniel, was born in October 2003. Her short stories have been published internationally in print magazines and online media, and even on coffee cans. Her nonfiction has been published in Ireland, the UK, America and Australia. She contributes a regular column to *Writer Online* and is a staff writer with *Netsurfer Digest*.

Philippa Tite
Breast is Best
Philippa Tite is the mother of six-year-old Christopher and one-year-old Jaden as well as being the wife of Chris (of indeterminate age). Currently living in KwaZulu-Natal, South Africa, and running a division of a computer company, she spends her free time doing her MBA and trying to juggle schedules. To pay for all these expensive habits (like children and MBA), she freelances for numerous papers and magazines covering diverse topics ranging from business strategy to child rearing. She is a fierce advocate against domestic violence and for South Africa.

Kira Vermond
Not as Advertised
Kira Vermond is a Toronto-based mom and freelance writer who still wonders if she'll ever get used to juggling laptop and baby. Her "money-work" can be found in *The Globe and Mail*, *Today's Parent* and more trade magazines than you can shake a rattle at. She and her husband, David, are raising their son, Nathan — who occasionally allows

his mom to have a shower long enough to shave both legs. He is truly her labor of love.

Peggy Vincent
If It Moves, Nurse It

Peggy Vincent, a retired midwife based in Berkeley, California, delivered nearly 3,000 babies during her career; nearly half were home births. Her memoir, *BABY CATCHER: Chronicles of a Modern Midwife*, was published by Scribner in 2002 and came out in paperback in 2003. A Los Angeles production company has optioned movie rights to the book. Peggy is now a full-time writer and lives at her home in Oakland, California with her husband and teenage son. Two adult children live nearby.

Diane Meredith Vogel
Babies and Boobies and Boisterous Boys, Oh My ...

Diane Meredith Vogel lives on a farm in Michigan with her husband/best friend. Her children are now grown and she has recently become a grandmother. With the nest empty, the couple is considering what adventures they will tackle in the future. Diane's writing has appeared in many periodicals and can also be found in two of the *Cup of Comfort* anthologies. She is currently working on a historical novel about the 1847 emigration of her Dutch ancestors. The book explores the difference between religion and true relationship with God. Besides writing, Diane enjoys painting and raising goats and dogs.

Yvonne Eve Walus
Sex, Lies and Measuring Tapes

Yvonne Eve Walus lives in New Zealand with her baby daughter, two cats (one of whom makes an excellent babysitter) and one husband (who's also not half-bad at babysitting). She did her first piece of creative writing when she was four years old, and never really stopped. Her daughter is making her first tentative steps in Mommy's footsteps and she loves all printed matter already.

Naida Lynn Wyckoff
"I Don't Know Nothin' 'Bout Birthin' Babies"

Naida Wyckoff resides in Virginia Beach, Virginia, with her husband of thirty-four years, Russell. In 1979, Naida graduated from Humboldt State University with a BA in fine arts. Her fabric art has warmed babies, graced churches and traveled the world. While Clover was her only "midwife" experience, she has had the privilege of witnessing six other births. Mother of a daughter and grandmother of four, she will always be an "Earth Mother" at heart.

Margaret Yang
Big Mama Underpants
Margaret Yang lives in Ann Arbor, Michigan, with her husband and two children. She is the restaurant critic for the *Ann Arbor Observer*. She is currently at work on her first novel.

About Viva Voce Press Inc.

Viva Voce Press Inc. is the owner of the trademark for *They Lied! True Tales of* ™. We publish collections of short stories based on stages and phases in life. We seek stories that will make the reader laugh out loud about situations in life that did not go as might have been expected. These are often the stories that might have seemed awkward or embarrassing at the time, but also suggested that at some point in the future they would provide rich fuel for laughter.

We gather stories through publicized calls for submissions. To see what themes we are currently working on, visit us at www.vivavocepress.com. Here you can also view our writers' guidelines for complete details on how and when to submit.

To order more copies of this book or others in our series as they are developed, visit your local bookstore or order directly at www.vivavocepress.com.

Theresa Kane, Publisher

Theresa Kane is an entrepreneur who specializes in communications. With an extensive background in marketing, communication and education projects, Theresa has brought her analytical skills, creativity and writing talent to a wide variety of campaigns. Whether to sell a product or motivate personal change, Theresa believes that clear communication is the first step.

As founder of Viva Voce Press Inc., Theresa continues to bring entrepreneurial spirit, leadership and energy to the team. The roots of this book can be traced to her genuine love of words and a long habit of listening for life's great moments captured in stories. Born at a baby shower eight years ago, *They Lied! True Tales of* ™ is proof that a good idea only gets stronger over time. With Viva Voce Press, she has the privilege of working with a creative team that is breaking the rules and writers who are sharing their quirky, funny moments with all of us.

Tamara Talbot, Creative Director

Tamara Talbot is a seasoned creative director who has a gift for delivering the best communication solutions. Her design and illustration talents bloomed while working in the publishing industry. Her work continues to prove successful in retail and corporate advertising, but her passion is in patient education and disease management. When she's not sweating over the drawing table, she's at home running after her two children — two young girls, who she's determined will become artists some day.

Gordon Kirkland, Senior Editor

Gordon Kirkland wears a number of hats in his working life. Here at Viva Voce Press Inc., he is the senior editor, bringing his comedic talents and book industry contacts to the team. He is also an award-winning author, syndicated columnist and conference speaker. He is a regular guest on radio and television shows in both Canada and the United States. He has been married to his first wife, Diane, for over thirty years. Together they have two grown sons, Mike and Brad, as well as Gordon's assistance dog, Tara, who helps him deal with the limitations brought on by a severe spinal injury.

Our latest call for submissions...

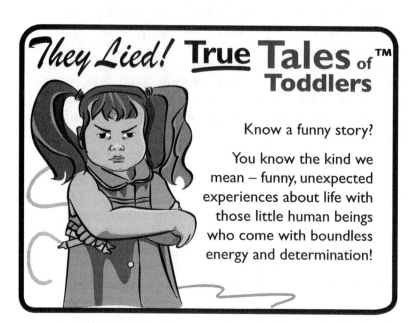

They Lied! **True** <u>**Tru**</u>**e Tales** of ™
Toddlers

Know a funny story?

You know the kind we mean – funny, unexpected experiences about life with those little human beings who come with boundless energy and determination!

They Lied! **True** <u>**Tru**</u>**e Tales** of ™
Weddings & Honeymoons

Know a funny story?
From off-beat engagements to ceremony surprises, reception dramas, to honeymoon disasters, we want to hear it all!

Do you have a story on Pregnancy, Childbirth or Breastfeeding?

Pregnancy is the oldest experience in the history of mankind.
But to anyone going through it,
it's THE first
and only
experience.

Our first call for submissions was so successful, we're now working on ...